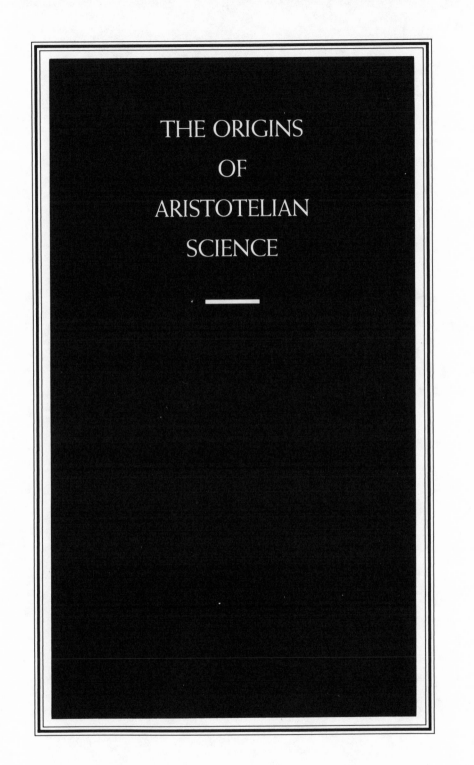

THE ORIGINS

OF

ARISTOTELIAN

SCIENCE

THE ORIGINS
OF
ARISTOTELIAN
SCIENCE

———

Michael Ferejohn

YALE UNIVERSITY PRESS

New Haven and London

Set in Linotron Sabon type by G & S Typesetters, Austin, Texas.

Printed in the United States of America by BookCrafters, Inc., Chelsea, Michigan.

Library of Congress Cataloging-in-Publication Data

Ferejohn, Michael T., 1945–
The origins of Aristotelian science / Michael T. Ferejohn.
p. cm.
Includes bibliographical references and index.
ISBN 0-300-04649-9 (alk. paper)
1. Aristotle—Contribution in theory of knowledge.   2. Aristotle—Contributions
in logic.   3. Knowledge, Theory of—History.   4. Logic, Ancient.   I. Title.
B491.K6F47 1991
121'.6'092—dc20   90-40942
CIP

The paper in this book meets the guidelines for permanence and durability of
the Committee on Production Guidelines for Book Longevity of the Council on
Library Resources.

10 9 8 7 6 5 4 3 2 1

To Donna

Contents

—

Acknowledgments

———

The first systematic work on this project was begun in 1981–82, while I held an Andrew W. Mellon Faculty Fellowship in the Humanities at Harvard. I am grateful to the Mellon foundation and Dr. Richard M. Hunt for their support during that year, and to the Harvard Philosophy Department for its kind hospitality. While there I benefited greatly from discussions on germinal ideas of the present work with John Murdoch, Martha Nussbaum, and Steven Strange. Since then I have received helpful comments and suggestions on earlier versions of various parts of the book from Robert Bolton, Daniel Devereux, Michael Frede, Cynthia Freeland, Robert McKay, Philip Rolnick, and Thomas Upton. Special thanks are due to David Charles and James Lennox, who read and commented on the entire manuscript. I especially want to thank my teachers, John Kekes, Nelson Pike, and Gerasimos Santas, for their unflagging encouragement and support during the difficult times, and Gregory Vlastos for showing me by his own example the close connection between good philosophy and good character. In the late stages of its preparation, the project has been facilitated by a number of Duke University Research Council Grants, and a Junior Faculty Research Leave in fall 1987.

THE ORIGINS
OF
ARISTOTELIAN
SCIENCE

———

Introduction

———

Books about Aristotle's *Posterior Analytics* have traditionally confined themselves to the ancient and respectable, yet relatively modest role of commentary.[1] Remarkably, there has yet to appear a full-scale account that even attempts to free itself from Aristotle's peculiar (perhaps even eccentric) order of exposition in this difficult work by placing all of its contents into a unified and intelligible analytical framework. Put simply, this is the void which the present work is intended to fill. In the most general terms, my aim here is to present and defend a comprehensive interpretation of the theory of "demonstrative knowledge" (ἡ ἀποδεικτικὴ ἐπιστήμη) as that theory is presented in the *Posterior Analytics* and selected parts of the *Prior Analytics*.

Now it is quite impossible to study any historical text except as a linguistic specimen without forming some definite view about the fundamental nature of the work it records. Therefore, our very first step should be to ask what sort of theory we are trying to understand. Here it is important to avoid the mistake, which is especially seductive in the case of Aristotle's *Analytics*, of supposing without adequate grounds that the intended subject of a text under study is alike in kind to that of intellectual endeavors current among one's own contemporaries. What makes this sort of anachronism all the more tempting in the case of the *Posterior Analytics* in particular is that one of the announced major topics of the work is referred to in numerous programmatic passages by the noun

[1]

ἐπιστήμη, which can be translated more or less accurately in some Aristotelian contexts as "science." When combined with the fact that Aristotle is deservedly renowned both as archetypical philosopher and as progenitor of many of the modern sciences, this can easily give rise to the idea that his treatise on ἐπιστήμη must fall within the field of philosophy of science as that description would be understood in modern contexts.

Tempting as it may be, this assimilation seriously misconstrues Aristotle's aims in this work. If by a "science" one means to denote a *scientific discipline*, that is, a discrete area of investigation or expertise delineated from others by having both a distinct subject matter and its own characteristic methods of investigation, then it is simply wrong to think that any such highly specialized concept is present from the outset of the *Posterior Analytics*. Instead, the treatise should be viewed as an occasion on which Aristotle begins to move toward an articulation of that concept. Hence, as my title is meant partly to suggest,[2] this book is not about Aristotelian science itself, but about how that very idea grew out of its philosophical antecedents.

At the same time, this is not to suggest that he ever achieves, or even approaches, full articulation of this concept in the *Posterior Analytics*. For while there are a number of passages where Aristotle can be seen distinguishing and even organizing ἐπιστῆμαι according to their subject matters,[3] nowhere in the work does he evince much theoretical interest in questions about how the practicing researcher of some area of study goes about (or should go about) collecting and organizing data or producing general results. In fact, the two *Analytics* on the whole seem to have very little to say about the investigatory methods of science in general, much less about any differences among those of the special sciences. Instead, these works proceed from the standpoint of a "finished" science whose research is complete, and are largely focused on questions about the characteristic patterns of reasoning through which one might prove, or "demonstrate" (ἀποδείκνυμι), that certain independently discovered particular facts of interest follow from, and are thus explained by, general scientific principles already in hand.[4]

But if it is granted that the treatise represents the initial stages of the movement toward the modern conception of a science, this raises the question of what provides the impetus for this movement in the first place. We will want to know what basic issues and problems lead Aristotle even to begin the process that culminated in the emergence of this technical concept. The key to this issue lies in acknowledging that there is an earlier usage of the term ἐπιστήμη, discernible in many of Plato's writings, which stands in rough alignment with that of the modern English noun "knowledge."[5] It will not be necessary to digress into a full-length philological study of this expression just to make my central point here, which is that the occurrences of ἐπιστήμη in the first three chapters of the *Posterior Analytics,* where the main topics of the book are introduced and motivated, conform generally to this earlier nontechnical usage, and so are better translated as "knowledge" than as "science." One good indication of this is the striking parallel between Aristotle's arguments in Book 1, Chapter 3 against various "nonfoundationalist" theories of justification and treatments of essentially the same topic found in recent epistemological literature. For the ultimate premises of those Aristotelian arguments flow out of certain reasonable pretheoretic ideas about the general nature of knowledge and justification, and not from any special features of the distinctively *Aristotelian* theory of "demonstrative knowledge" (ἀποδεικτικὴ ἐπιστήμη) whose presentation officially begins in Chapter 4.

But if it is wrong to construe the main subject of the *Posterior Analytics* as philosophy of science, it would be equally mistaken to classify the work as a piece of general epistemology. While it is true that Aristotle begins his treatise with a discussion of what he sees as certain general constraints on any adequate theory of knowledge, it is also true that this initial stage of his inquiry is extremely short-lived. From there he moves swiftly, beginning in Book 1, Chapter 4, to the task of actually constructing an account (based on his own theory of syllogistic deduction) of "knowledge in the unqualified sense" (ἐπιστήμη ἁπλῶς) that he believes successfully meets these constraints.

This overview of the *Analytics* as located within, and partially traversing, the area between general epistemology and philosophy of science, informs most of the material in this book. Each chapter is organized around an attempt to show how one or more of Aristotle's general philosophical views on the nature of knowledge and its neighboring concepts ultimately contributes in important ways to the theory of demonstrative knowledge which he ultimately develops.

There is, however, a sense in which the *Posterior Analytics* has something of an amalgamated character, and this will add a further complication to the proceedings. As so often happens, Aristotle is evidently concerned in this area to make his own independently developed views consistent and coherent with what he sees as right or redeemable in Platonism. For this reason, some of the prefiguring views to be discussed below are positions simply taken over from Plato without visible demurrer, while others are distinctively Aristotelian in origin, and in some cases even anti-Platonic in spirit. A large part of my aim here, then, is to show how Aristotle's theory of demonstrative knowledge is generated out of a confluence of his own original thought with philosophical views inherited from the Academy.

There is one final aspect of the *Posterior Analytics* which should be introduced as a preliminary matter. Given Aristotle's notorious promiscuous movement between the formal and material modes of speech, it would be difficult to characterize his philosophical methodology as having made what has been called in this century "the linguistic turn." That said, there is nonetheless substantial point and profit in noticing that his general theoretical approach in many of the so-called logical works of the *Organon* has features in common with that of contemporary philosophical logic. To be sure, he never formulates explicitly, nor does he religiously observe, any hard and fast distinction between *sentences* on the one hand and the extralinguistic *facts* or *propositions* they might be thought to express on the other. All the same, he often finds it important and useful to select and prefer what he evidently regards as the most metaphysically perspicuous ways of expressing certain kinds of facts, and to that extent he seems committed, at least implicitly, to something like a doctrine of "logical form." What is even more to the present point, there are a number of passages in the early works (most especially, the *Categories, De Interpretatione,* and the *Posterior Analytics*) that are best understood as part of an ongoing effort on Aristotle's part to work out the details of a *theory of predication.* As it will apply here, this means that most or all of what Aristotle says about the nature of scientific knowledge in the *Posterior Analytics* can be cast without intolerable distortion into talk about the requisite features of the kinds of statements he thinks suitable for expressing or conveying such knowledge. Accordingly, the formative effects of his various philosophical commitments on his theory of demonstrative knowledge will fall out below as a set of syntactic and semantic restrictions on what he will allow as legitimate scientific predications.

The broad context of part 1 of this book, "The Structure of Demonstration," is dominated by the arguments in *Posterior Analytics,* Book 1, Chapter 3, mentioned earlier for the following thesis:

> (A1) Any genuine system of justification must be
> foundational.

Specifically, it will be argued in chapter 1, "Demonstration, Division, and the Syllogism," that this foundationalist position actually has two quite distinct, though easily confused, consequences for Aristotle's theory of scientific knowledge. In the first place, inasmuch as the logical machinery of demonstration is provided by the theory of the syllogism presented in the first book of the *Prior Analytics*, (A1) requires that the demonstration of any given explicandum must rest ultimately on statements that are not themselves derived syllogistically from still more basic premises. Predictably, Aristotle identifies the feature responsible for an ultimate premise being "syllogistically primitive" in this way as its being "immediate" (ἄμεσος), by which is meant that there is no middle term that can be interposed to form a mediated predicational link between its subject and predicate terms. Out of this naturally emerges his view that each demonstrative science has associated with it a distinctive set of statements that are immediate in just this sense and therefore function as the "primary premises" (πρῶτον προτάσεις) out of which all syllogistic demonstrations within that science are constructed.

However, in addition to this intrascientific type of foundationalism, which is clearly linked to the syllogistic requirements of the *Aristotelian* theory of demonstration, I will argue that there is another more general *epistemological* foundationalism also present in the *Posterior Analytics*, and the tendency to confuse the two has confounded many ancient and modern attempts to comprehend the work. This second position is that a demonstrative science (or indeed any genuine justificatory system), now taken as a whole (primary premises included), must proceed from "starting points" (ἀρχαί) that themselves are not, and cannot be, proper parts of that science. This is just to say that by virtue of the very nature of justification, no scientific enterprise could possibly function as a bootstrap operation somehow capable of generating or grounding results ex nihilo. Rather, Aristotle insists, it can be entered into only by an epistemic subject who is already in possession of an adequate stock of preexistent (that is to say, prescientific) knowledge not itself in need of justification.

Some recent writers have tried without much success to equate these external *epistemological* starting points of a demonstrative science as a whole with the internal *logical* starting points—primary premises—of individual syllogistic demonstrations within a science, and it must be admitted that this idea has been encouraged to some extent by Aristotle himself. Against this mistaken view, which I call "strict syllogisticism," I shall argue for a two-stage interpretation of demonstrative science.[6] On this account, the construction of scientific explanations begins with what

I call a *framing stage*, which will be represented as a nonsyllogistic procedure descended from the Platonic method of "division" (διαίρεσις) in which the primary premises of a demonstrative science are generated out of the epistemological starting points pertinent to the science in question. This is then followed by a *syllogistic stage* in which these primary premises are deployed in the syllogistic derivations of particular facts to be explained by that science.[7]

Of the various sorts of starting points actually discussed by Aristotle in *Posterior Analytics* 1.2 and 1.10, some (for example, generic existence assumptions, and the "logical" principle of Noncontradiction) will be interpreted in chapter 1 as nothing more than nonsubstantive background assumptions that can be seen independently to be necessary for any divisional procedure, Platonic, Aristotelian, or otherwise. Chapter 2, "Demonstration and Definition," will then focus narrowly and exclusively on the all-important *substantive* assumptions employed in the framing stage, namely the Aristotelian "definitions" (ὅροι or ὁρίσμοι) that convey immediate connections between terms. It will be argued that Aristotle's complex attitude towards ὅροι is precipitated by a desire to make his theory of predication conform both to the Platonic epistemological principles:

> (P1) Genuine knowledge must be of what is universal

and

> (P2) There can be no knowledge of particulars,

and to his own radically anti-Platonic metaphysical theses:

> (A2) The things which are most real are (particular) primary substances

and

> (A3) There can be no "separated" universals.

These seemingly incongruous commitments lead him to identify (or invent) as the paradigm for scientific predications a rather curious type of statement that I characterize as the *referential universal*. A sentence of this type is universal in form, but unlike its Post-Fregean counterpart, existentially loaded in the sense that it involves distributed reference to all of the particulars that fall under its subject term, and so entails or presupposes their existence. As they will be explicated here, Aristotelian ὅροι will then turn out to resemble primary premises *syntactically* in that both are universal statements that express immediate connections between terms. On the other hand, the two types of statements will also be distinguished from one another on *semantic* grounds because ὅροι do not involve any reference to particulars (and hence are not *referential* universals), but are instead free-floating, or Platonistic, universal predications that could be true even in a universe containing no mundane particulars whatever. Along the way, I will also argue that this crucial distinction between Platonistic definitions and referential universal immediate premises is a central element in Aristotle's subtle and complicated final position in *Posterior Analytics* 2.7–10 on the question of whether, and in what sense, definitions are demonstrable.

By the end of part 1 it should be clear that Aristotle characterizes the final products of demonstration as knowledge *in the strictest sense possible* for two complementary reasons, both of which stem ultimately from features of the framing stage of demonstration. In the first place, as has already been remarked, unlike the ὅροι that go into this procedure, the primary premises that come out of it, and therefore the explicanda that follow from those premises, are all referential universals, and so are about the most real objects in Aristotle's early ontology. But more than that, it will also be seen that the framing stage also systematizes the subject-genus of a demonstrative science insofar as the set of primary premises it yields can be thought to represent a taxonomic ordering of that genus by the immediate connections expressed by those premises. But this means that the whole procedure of constructing an Aristotelian demonstration does not just explain facts individually; it also locates the explained fact within the appropriate structured field of scientific interest. This brings Aristotle's theory into line with an attractive epistemological position prominent in the final part of Plato's *Theaetetus*:

> (P3) One cannot possess knowledge of a particular fact
> without possessing knowledge of the entire system
> of facts of which it is an element.

Part 2 is a close study of Aristotle's views concerning the specific sorts of immediate connections he is willing to permit between the terms of acceptable demonstrative premises. The main point of departure for this study is Aristotle's endorsement of yet another familiar Platonic epistemological requirement:

> (P4) Knowledge is of what cannot be otherwise,

and its nearly immediate consequences that the conclusions, and a fortiori, the premises, of scientific demonstrations must in some sense or other be necessary. This endorsement leads Aristotle to require not only that his theory of predication provide conditions of truth, but also that it make a distinction between those statements whose truth is a matter of mere happenstance (which therefore, presumably, are not subject to scientific explanation) and others whose truth is a matter of necessity (and which therefore do fall properly within the domain of Aristotelian science).

In fact, I shall argue that the *Organon* contains two distinct theories of predication which reflect this distinction, and that these two theories differ drastically in their overall sophistication and their sensitivity to significant differences among the types of statements they treat. One of these, which I claim is only implicit in the first five chapters of the *Categories,* will be exposed in chapter 3 as a relatively simple theory that in the end does no better than to provide a set of necessary (but not sufficient) categorial conditions for necessary truth. Against this background, Aristotle will be portrayed in chapter 4 as making another, more subtle, approach to the same topic in Book 1, Chapter 4 of the *Posterior Analytics.* In particular, he is there able to provide *sufficient* conditions for necessary truth by bringing into play an idea that is barely embryonic in the *Categories* (but that eventually blossoms into one of his most important metaphysical doctrines), namely that for every general (natural) kind of thing, there corresponds a unique cluster of characteristics essential to (and in some sense even responsible for) something's belonging to that kind. In later works, such clusters are referred to variously by the use of such terms as "nature" (φύσις), "essence" (τὸ τί ἦν εἶναι), and "substance" (οὐσία), but Aristotle's preferred means of designating them in the *Organon* is with the simple nominalized interrogative, "*the what-is-it*" (τὸ τί ἐστι). The fundamental distinction between properties that are within the what-is-it of a thing and others that are not then forms the conceptual basis for a theory of predication in *Posterior Analytics* 1.4 that distinguishes necessary, "per se" (καθ'αὐτό), predications, which are the proper concern of demonstrative science, from merely contingent, "*per accidens*" (κατὰ συμβεβηκός), truths that lie outside its domain.

In chapter 5 it will be argued further that because Aristotle takes over a certain Platonic view about definition,

> (P5) A definition involves the specification of a genus
> and a differentia,

his new theory of predication gives a separate analysis for another group of necessary premises, namely those involving the predication of differentiae, which do not fit comfortably within the simpler theory of the *Cate-*

gories. In addition, the theory of the *Posterior Analytics* will be seen in chapter 6 to make further advances over that of the *Categories* by extending the range of scientifically respectable truths to include, as an additional type of per se premise, predications of what are called in the *Topics* "properties," or "propria" (ἴδια), statements expressing causal (as opposed to "analytic") connections, and even certain general statements that seemingly do not express invariable connections, but are merely true "for the most part" (ἐπὶ τὸ πολύ). In contrast to these relaxations of his requirements for scientific premises, Aristotle's discussion of one other sense of the term per se in *Posterior Analytics* 1.4 will be interpreted as an attempt to exclude from his theory a certain sort of apparently significant predication that is also left entirely out of account in the *Categories.*

Chapter 7, "Demonstration and Negation," concerns the question of how negation (or more precisely, negative predication) figures in the theory of demonstrative knowledge given in the *Posterior Analytics.* We shall see that, while Aristotle has a theoretical need to include such predications as legitimate demonstrative premises, he also has good philosophical reasons to be troubled by their presence. He is uncomfortably aware of Plato's efforts in the *Sophist* and elsewhere to rescue the concept of negation from the "Parmenidean" indictment that its use inevitably leads into deep and inescapable paradox. More specifically, I shall argue that one of these alleged paradoxes in particular involves what I call the problem of "semantic fragmentation." This is a certain *meaning defect* which Plato believes to come out of employing negative predicates as "indefinite" (ἀόριστον) terms in contexts where they are supposed to denote unrestricted (or insufficiently restricted) complements of what is denoted by the positive predicates they contain. On the account to be given here, Aristotle follows Plato not only in seeing semantic fragmentation as a serious threat to the possibility of negative predication, but also in accepting the specific diagnosis of it given in the *Sophist* as due to underrestriction. That is to say, he is committed in the *Analytics* to two additional Platonic theses:

> (P6) Negative predicates denoting underrestricted complements are semantically fragmented;
>
> (P7) Terms which are semantically fragmented are meaningless.

With this diagnosis, the solution to the difficulty is obvious: simply make sure your theory of predication does not permit the occurrence of negative predicates except where their denotations are sufficiently restricted.

Aristotle's way of achieving this, which is our special concern here, is in effect to compartmentalize the whole field of demonstrative science into the so-called special sciences. He does this by requiring that each ἐπιστήμη be pertinent to a unique genus of things which it studies and that the demonstrations of that ἐπιστήμη contain no term (positive or negative) whose denotation is not wholly included within that genus.

Since this book is limited in scope to a discussion of the interconnections among the logical, metaphysical, and epistemological doctrines of Aristotle's early works (especially those of the *Analytics*), I shall avoid making reference to his later writings except for purposes of illustration or merely circumstantial textual argumentation. However, I should close these introductory remarks by mentioning two familiar issues in Aristotelian scholarship that will not be pursued here. First, it will not be asked whether the theory of predication set out in the *Posterior Analytics* suffers any substantial revision by the time Aristotle writes the notorious middle books (E–Θ) of the *Metaphysics*. More specifically, I shall not attempt here to decide whether his eventual attachment to the matter-form analysis of substances (which is conspicuously absent from the *Organon*) eventually requires him to repudiate, or merely to extend, his earlier theory in order to analyze "predications" expressing the new-found relation of material constitution. Second, nothing will be said here on the undeniably important question of whether the a priori theory of demonstrative science presented in the *Analytics* is in the end compatible with theoretical remarks about explanation or actual explanatory practice in Aristotle's later scientific (especially his biological) works. Again, this book is intended as a study of the *origins* of Aristotelian science, not of what it eventually becomes. The rationale for both of these omissions is essentially the same: part of my aim here is to counteract what I perceive as recent popular tendencies in both of these areas to read Aristotle "backwards" by being too eager to find in the earlier works signs of complications and difficulties in his views that do not in fact become evident until later in the Corpus. In saying this, I certainly do not mean to deny that there are ever occasions on which Aristotle says less than he believes about peripheral (or for that matter, central) problems and issues raised by the doctrines he expounds. But even so, I believe it is necessary to approach a difficult work like the *Posterior Analytics* in the first instance *on its own terms* by trying to understand it as presenting an intelligible and essentially self-contained theory, and not merely as a superficial and inadequate preview of later, deeper, and more subtle doctrines that it does not actually discuss. Indeed, without such a free-standing interpretation of the *Posterior Analytics* that respects its integrity as an independent work, I find it hard to see how one could even form (much less answer) meaningful questions about whether or how its doctrines are modified, extended, or abandoned in later treatises.

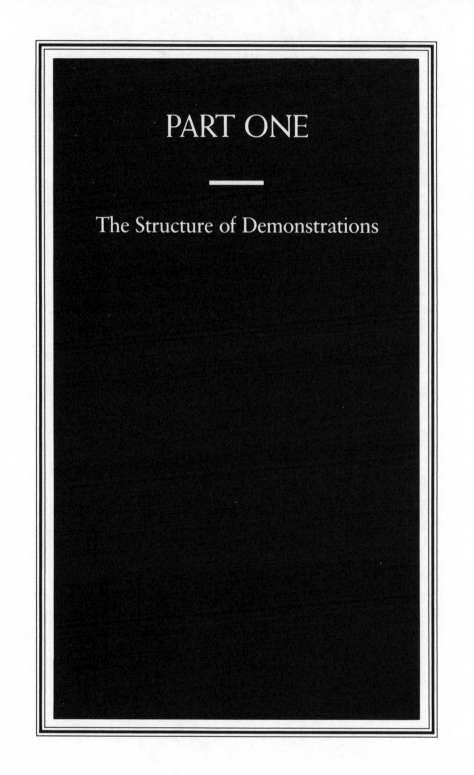

PART ONE

—

The Structure of Demonstrations

ONE

━━━

Demonstration, Division, and the Syllogism

It would perhaps not be too far wrong to describe the *Posterior Analytics* as an ugly stepchild in the Aristotelian corpus. Since ancient times the work has suffered from a reputation for being unpolished in style, tentative in tone, and even lacking in organization, judgments which have served their makers as an excuse to pick and choose the parts of the treatise they find intelligible, interesting, and important, and to disregard other parts as so much confused exposition on the part of Aristotle or his transcribers. One particularly unfortunate outgrowth of this attitude has been the idea that to look for a comprehensive framework that organizes all the apparently diverse discussions occurring in the work is to conduct a hopeless search for something that simply is not there.

In the introduction to his 1949 edition of the *Analytics,* Sir David Ross offered quite plausible mitigation for defects in the style and tone of the work, respectively, by pointing out that there is a reasonably wide variation, having very little to do with content, in the degree to which different Aristotelian treatises are "ready for press," and that the intrinsic difficulty of the topics treated by the *Posterior Analytics* (compared, for example, to the *Prior Analytics*) in any event makes it very easy to understand why Aristotle should express the views developed there in cautious and tentative language. Here I propose to answer the remaining complaint, that the work is disorganized, by arguing that the *Posterior Ana-*

lytics is in fact constructed around a quite powerful (if not always perfectly visible) organizational scheme. On the view I shall be advancing, the treatise is not simply a loosely connected set of local discussions on a very broad and undefined group of topics. Instead, it can be understood as a systematic attempt by Aristotle to give and defend answers to two very closely related questions that naturally flow out of an investigatory current stemming from Plato's *Meno* and running through his *Republic* and *Theaetetus:* first, what are the essential features of "knowledge in the unqualified sense" (ἐπιστήμη ἁπλῶς), that is, the very highest and most secure form of knowledge available to humans, and second, how can these features be secured within the context of Aristotle's own logic and theory of predication?

More particularly, I suggest that Aristotle treats the first of these two questions in the opening three chapters of the *Posterior Analytics*, thus developing a set of desiderata which he believes any plausible theory of ἐπιστήμη ἁπλῶς must satisfy, and then spends virtually the rest of the work showing that a theory of his own invention in fact does so.[1]

DEMONSTRATION, SYLLOGISM, AND
THE FOUNDATIONS OF KNOWLEDGE

Not coincidentally, what is by far the most striking and important of these desiderata makes its appearance in the very first sentence of the opening chapter of the work: "All learning and all teaching of the discursive sort arises out of preexistent knowledge" (*Posterior Analytics* 1.1.71a1–2).

With its specific reference to "teaching" (διδασκαλία) and "learning" (μάθησις), this remark sounds a theme that must have been calculated to evoke comparisons with Plato's introduction at *Meno* 85D–E of the doctrine of ἀνάμνησις as a solution to the famous paradox about the possibility of learning formulated earlier in the dialogue at 80D–E. In chapter 2 I will argue that these Platonic overtones are meant partly to motivate a distinction between universal and particular knowledge which will turn out to be an absolutely pivotal element in Aristotle's own theory. For now, however, it will suffice to notice two outstanding features of the very special way in which Aristotle himself understands this remark. One is that Aristotle, unlike Plato in Book 6 of *The Republic*, is here identifying the highest form of knowledge as one that is "discursive" (διανοητική) in nature, which means that it is a sort grounded on "reasoned justification." This thought becomes clear later on in Chapter 2 when he describes "knowledge in the unqualified sense" (ἐπιστήμη ἁπλῶς) as a sort that arises "through demonstration" (δι' ἀποδείξεως), and is picked up in *Posterior Analytics* 1.13 and again in *Posterior Analytics* 2.1 and 2.2, where the point is made that it is one thing to know *that* a certain fact holds (that is, to know "that it is" [τὸ ὅτι]), and another (presumably better) thing to know *that on account of which* it obtains (that is, its τὸ διότι) by providing a demonstration that elucidates its causes (2.1.89b30–1; 2.2.89b35–90a5). The other point, which might reasonably be thought to follow from this, and which Aristotle takes pains to defend in *Posterior Analytics* 1.3, is that the possibility of such discursive knowledge requires that it must arise ultimately out of a nondiscursive, or undemonstrated, form of knowledge possessed beforehand.[2] But where Plato draws the notorious inference in the *Meno* that such preexistent knowledge must be inborn or innate, Aristotle is content with the more moderate position that this preexistent knowledge must simply be at hand prior to the actual demonstrations of the discursive knowledge that rests upon it. In short, then, this very central desideratum of Aristotle's theory of the highest form of knowledge is that the justification of such knowledge must be *foundational* in the sense that it must rest ultimately on preexistent first principles, and generate a body of discursive knowledge from these.

It is well known that the logic by which demonstrative knowledge is generated out of preexistent first principles in Aristotle's own theory is supposed to be provided by the theory of the syllogism in the *Prior Analytics*. This, however, presents immediate problems in identifying precisely what these first principles might be. In particular, the difficulty is precipitated by the existence of two substantial groups of texts which seem to point in opposing exegetical directions. On one hand, there are a good many passages (hereafter referred to as group A) in both the *Prior* and *Posterior Analytics* that suggest an extremely tight linkage between the notions of ἀπόδειξις and συλλογισμός, to the extent that an Aristotelian science seems to be depicted in them as a sort of proto-Euclidean axiomatic system that starts from a relatively small set of "starting points" (ἀρχαί) or "assumptions" (λαμβανόμενα), and then proceeds by means of purely deductive (that is to say, syllogistic) inference-chains to "prove" all of the explicanda pertinent to that science. The passages in this group fall into three distinct subgroups. There are first of all those in which Aristotle says explicitly that a demonstration is a kind of syllogism (*Prior*

Analytics 1.4.25b26; *Posterior Analytics* 1.2.71b17), or in other ways makes it clear that the two subjects are very intimately connected (*Prior Analytics* 1.1.24a10; *Posterior Analytics* 1.2.72a10–15; 2.19.99b15). Secondly, there are places where demonstration is linked to the "figures" (σχήματα) of the syllogism (*Posterior Analytics* 1.13.78b13ff), most especially the first (*Posterior Analytics* 1.14.79a17). Finally, a number of passages appear to equate the construction of a demonstration with the interposition of a "middle term" (μέσον) between two others already noticed to be connected somehow (*Posterior Analytics* 2.2 passim; 1.13.78b3ff).

Quite aside from whether this geometrical conception agrees with present-day understandings of the logic of scientific explanation, the problem is that it seems not to fit very well with Aristotle's own remarks concerning the details of his theory. Such a tight connection between demonstration and syllogism would seem to place very definite syllogistic constraints on both the form and interpretation of the ἀρχαί and the λαμβανόμενα of science. Yet even a quick study of the passages (here called group B) where Aristotle identifies and discusses these items indicates what seem to be frequent and flagrant violations of these constraints. These passages are mostly contained in the first eleven chapters of the *Posterior Analytics,* with the highest concentrations in the second and tenth. Of special concern here will be Aristotle's discussions of "definitions" (ὅρος or ὁρισμός; 1.2.72a15–25; 1.10.76b35), "common [axioms]" (τὰ κοινά; 1.10.76a40; 1.11.77a10–35), "assumptions of existence" (ὅτι ἔστι; 1.10.76a31–7; 76b3–23), and "assumptions of meaning" (τί σημαίνει; 1.10.76a31–7; 76b3–23).

The apparent incompatibility between these two groups of passages has provoked two extreme forms of reactions among Aristotle's interpreters. Those whom I shall call the *strict syllogisticists* take very seriously the geometrical conception suggested by group A and consequently try to understand the texts in group B in a way that gives to the various kinds of ἀρχαί and λαμβανόμενα discussed therein an aura of syllogistic respectability. On the other side there are the *antisyllogisticists*, who, upon noting the contortions through which the strict syllogisticists put the texts of group B, propose to give up entirely the idea that demonstration is significantly based on the theory of the syllogism presented in the *Prior Analytics,* despite Aristotle's clear declarations in group A to the contrary.[3]

My general view is that each side of this debate is mistaken for failing to take into account a large portion of what Aristotle actually says about the subject at issue.[4] This fault is not shared by the interpretation to be defended here, which might be thought of as a qualified form of syllogisticism. According to this account, Aristotle does indeed (as the passages in group A suggest) regard demonstration as essentially and importantly syllogistic in character, yet he is not committed to the proposition (falsified by group B) that all of the ἀρχαί and λαμβανόμενα of demonstration are ultimate premises in syllogistic justification-chains. More specifically, my central proposal is that (a) the whole process of Aristotelian ἀπόδειξις is a two-stage affair, (b) only the second of these is syllogistic in nature (although it is strictly so), and (c) many of the ἀρχαί and λαμβανόμενα of Aristotelian science play out their roles in the initial, presyllogistic stage (or, as I shall call it, the "framing" stage) of demonstration.

DEMONSTRATION AND DIVISION: THE FRAMING STAGE

The key to understanding the logical structure of Aristotelian demonstration comes with an adequate appreciation of its architect's ambivalence toward the method of "division" (διαίρεσις) practiced by Plato[5] and other members of his Academy.[6] To begin with, it is generally recognized that *Posterior Analytics* 2.5 and *Prior Analytics* 1.31 both record a critical attitude on Aristotle's part toward this Platonic method insofar as it was advanced as a method of proof intended to rival his own method of demonstration.[7] He argues in both places that if an individual step in the divisional process (wherein some predesignated target is sequentially located on one side or the other of finer and finer differentiations) were to be construed as an attempt at logical inference, it would have to be judged invalid.[8] So, for instance, in *Prior Analytics* 1.31 he considers the following sequence of divisional steps,

Step N

(1) Every man is animal, and
(2) every animal is mortal or immortal, so
(3) every man is mortal or immortal.
In particular,
(4) Every man is mortal (animal),

Step N + 1

(5) Every mortal (animal) is footed or footless, and
(4) every man is mortal (animal), so

(6) Every man is footed or footless.

More particularly,

(7) Every man is footed.

and argues (a) that the so-called conclusion of each step ([4] and [7], the statement carried over to the succeeding step) is never actually proved from earlier lines, but is instead simply introduced in each case as a new and unsupported assumption (46.b12.18–19),⁹ and (b) that even though the disjunctive predications in each step ([3] and [6]) do follow logically from prior statements ([1] with [2], and [5] with [4], respectively), these inferences cannot be cases of demonstration because they violate the rule that any demonstration of a universal affirmative must be in Barbara, and so must have a middle which is included in its major term (46a39–b4).¹⁰

But while it is generally acknowledged that Aristotle is hostile for these reasons to διαίρεσις if and when it is proposed as a self-sufficient method of proof, it is not always noticed that in both *Analytics* (especially in *Posterior Analytics* 2.13) he actually advocates the use of something very much like this Platonic device, provided that certain safeguards are observed, for a very specific and limited purpose within his own account of the demonstrative generation of the highest form of knowledge. Thus, at *Posterior Analytics* 2.13.96b15 he says that when one is "making a systematic study" (πραγματεύηται) of some subject (presumably with the aim of developing unqualified knowledge), it is "necessary" (χρή) to "divide" (διελεῖν) the genus into its primary, "atomic" (ἄτομον) species. The same point is then made even more explicit at b25 when Aristotle allows that "divisions according to differentiae" (αἱ δὲ διαιρέσεις αἱ κατὰ τὰς διαφοράς) are "useful" (χρήσιμοι) in such investigations.¹¹ Furthermore, *Prior Analytics* 1.27–31 sheds some light on the specific function this procedure is supposed to serve within the demonstrative process, since it is presented in those chapters as part of a wider discussion about how, as Aristotle's foundationalism and logical theory requires, one can and should go about selecting appropriate premises of syllogisms in general, and appropriate ultimate premises of demonstrative syllogisms in particular.¹²

It is important, however, not to expect more of these chapters than they are intended to accomplish. A well-known passage in *Posterior Analytics* 1.2 sets out six different conditions that a demonstrative premise must meet: "Now if knowing is as we have laid down, demonstrative knowledge must come from [premises] which are (a) *true*, (b) *primary*, (c) *immediate*, (d) *better known* than, (e) *prior* to, and (f) *causative* of, the conclusion" (71b16–20). It would be a mistake simply to assume that if *Posterior Analytics* 2.13 and *Prior Analytics* 1.27–32 give us a method for collecting premises that have these characteristics, then the method in question is one that *selects for* all of these characteristics. Indeed, quite to the contrary, I shall argue presently that the divisional method promoted in these chapters is one for assuring the satisfaction of conditions (b) and (c) alone.

To begin with, truth, the first condition listed at 71b16, is no more than an unanalyzable consequence of Aristotle's very minimal requirement that a demonstration must constitute a proof (or sound argument) for its conclusion. For it is hard to imagine that anything illuminating could be said about how one should go about finding true statements that would not proceed by saying how to find statements that have certain sorts of justifications, or perhaps have certain intrinsic features which exempt them from justification. On the other hand, it seems that much more can and should be said about the final three requirements: that the premises of a demonstration must be (d) "better known than" (γνωριμωτέρων), (e) "prior to" (προτέρων), and (f) "causative of" (αἰτίων) the conclusion. For even though these are all given as relative conditions (that is, as conditions that the premises of a single demonstrative syllogism must have relative to the conclusion of that syllogism), Aristotle's syllogistic foundationalism entails that a complete syllogistic demonstration must rest ultimately on premises that are "*most* knowable," (epistemologically) *primary*, and *causally basic*. These absolute conditions taken together are supposed to constitute the all-important connecting points between metaphysics and epistemology needed to redeem Aristotle's fundamental presumption that a demonstration must not just prove its conclusion, but also explain its truth. In other words, as he sometimes puts it, a demonstration must not merely show *that* (ὅτι) the demonstrated proposition is true, but also *why* (διότι) it is true (*Posterior Analytics* 1.2.71b9–19, 2.2.89b35–90a5).[13] Therefore, if Aristotle wants finally to represent his theory of ἀπόδειξις as an account of scientific explanation—again, in an objective sense[14]—he must eventually say what it is about ultimate demonstrative premises that enables them to satisfy conditions (d)–(f) relative to *all* the conclusions they support, and thus to function as the foundational elements in a system of objective explanation.

My central aim in part 2 will be to argue that the pivotal chapter in this project is *Posterior Analytics* 1.4, where Aristotle maintains that all three of these crucial conditions on demonstrative premises can be secured by the single, though complex, requirement that all such premises be instances of what he calls "per se" (καθ'αὑτό) predication. Moreover, it will also emerge during that discussion that this key expression, like so many other important pieces of Aristotle's philosophical terminology, is "said in many ways" (πολλαχῶς λέγεται), and that, as a result, the multiple explications it receives in *Posterior Analytics* 1.4 can be seen to function as something like a catalogue of correspondingly different types of nonaccidental connections that Aristotle allows to hold between the terms of legitimate scientific predications.

But this must come later. For though even at this early stage it is hard to overstate the importance of these issues to Aristotle's theory as a whole, the truth is that he simply ducks them in the chapters presently under discussion, where he is concerned exclusively with the broad structure of demonstration. Thus, in *Prior Analytics* 1.27 he insists at 43b7–11 that in order to select demonstrative premises correctly it is necessary already to have distinguished between the accidental and different sorts of nonaccidental attributes [15] of a given subject, but he says nothing about how this distinction might be accomplished. And likewise in *Posterior Analytics* 2.13, when he declares at 97a24 that one of the three rules to observe in following his recommended procedure is to "grasp attributes in the what-is-it" (τοῦ λαβεῖν τὰ κατηγορούμενα ἐν τῷ τί ἐστι) of the subject, he again offers no guidance on how such attributes are to be distinguished from other types.

In order to understand this silence, we have to keep in mind that when Aristotle claims in *Prior Analytics* 1.27–32 and *Posterior Analytics* 2.13 that the operation he describes as "division according to differentiae" at 96b25–6 is a useful (and even necessary [16]) device for the acquisition of the ultimate premises of demonstration, what he is promoting is not actually Platonic Division itself, but rather a certain distinctively Aristotelian adaptation of that method. For even though the two procedures bear a strong structural resemblance to one another (they both proceed by "dividing a genus down into its indivisible species," in the exact language of *Posterior Analytics* 96b15), this should not obscure the fact that they also have vastly different epistemological functions within their respective systems. As it presented in the *Sophist* and elsewhere, there is not much doubt that Platonic Division is regarded by its author as a complete (that is to say, self-sufficient) philosophical method for producing or discovering a desired definition (specifically that of the indivisible kind predesignated as the target of the division). [17] Not only that, but it is also evident from *Sophist* 253C–E that Plato sees the prosecution of the method as the proper business of the very highest form of intellectual activity (which he refers to alternately in that passage as "dialectic" and "philosophy"), and that he consequently views the definitions generated by the method as the proper objects of the highest epistemic attitude countenanced in his system: knowledge, in the strictest possible Platonic sense of the term.

Now, as it will be interpreted here, the Aristotelian adaptation of Platonic Division advocated in *Posterior Analytics* 2.13 and *Prior Analytics* 1.27–32 differs from its distinguished ancestor in both of these respects. In the next chapter we shall try to ascertain exactly what it is about the logical character of definitions generated by Platonic Division that inclines Aristotle to deny them the status of knowledge in *his* strictest sense of the term. However, the most immediate and striking point of difference between the two methods is that Aristotle's version, unlike Plato's, is not a method for *generating* definitions, but instead one whose use presupposes that one has somehow already grasped an appropriate set of immediate principles (some, but not all, of which are definitions[18]), and which then deploys these principles over some field of scientific interest (in Aristotle's technical usage, a *genus*) in such a way as to collect the ultimate syllogistic premises required to construct demonstrative syllogisms, and so to develop a systematic understanding (or knowledge *simpliciter*) concerning that field. Consequently, where Plato is able to conceive of definitions as the products of an entirely self-sufficient philosophical method (dialectic), and so as specimens of the highest form of knowledge, for Aristotle they function as mere starting points: part of the preexistent material, called for by *Posterior Analytics* 1.1 and 2, from which knowledge simpliciter—or demonstrative knowledge—is ultimately generated.

This difference from Plato is somewhat obscured by the second sentence of *Posterior Analytics* 2.13 (96a22–23), where Aristotle says that his concern in the upcoming chapter will be to explain how one should "hunt out" (θηρεύειν) "attributes in the what-is-it" (τὰ ἐν τῷ τί ἐστι κατηγορούμενα). This certainly makes it appear that what is to follow will be a discussion of how the elements of definitions can be discovered. This appearance proves to be deceptive, however, since the exact parallel in language between this remark and 97b7–11 entails that the subject of *Posterior Analytics* 2.13 as a whole cannot be how to discover τὰ ἐν τῷ τί ἐστι κατηγορούμενα. For as we have just seen, the later passage tells us that a precondition of success for the method under discussion is that one must *already* have the ability to grasp those very attributes. And in fact, we know independently that the question of how the definitional starting points of ἀπόδειξις are initially apprehended is put off until the notoriously difficult final chapter of the entire treatise (Book 2, Chapter 19), whose details will be dealt with below in chapter 2. By contrast, as I have suggested, this issue is simply finessed by Aristotle in *Prior Analytics* 1.27–32 and *Posterior Analytics* 2.13 when he issues offhand admonitions that the procedure he is recommending must restrict itself to *essential* (or at the very least, nonaccidental[19]) connections between terms without offering the slightest advice in either place on how this restriction might be ensured.

I have been arguing that, because the method of "*Aristotelian* division" advocated in these chapters does not provide (and indeed presupposes) a way of distinguishing essential (or nonaccidental) from accidental predications, then, since this distinction is what ultimately grounds conditions (d)–(f) at *Posterior Analytics* 71b16–22, it follows that the method is not designed to test for those conditions. But if, as I asserted above, there is no independent test for condition (a), truth, we may then ask, what *is* the method supposed to accomplish? According to the interpretation I propose, it is offered by Aristotle as a way of obtaining premises that satisfy the remaining two requirements listed at 71b16–20, namely that demonstrative premises be (b) "*primary*" (πρῶτον) in the sense of being (c) "*immediate*" (ἄμεσον).

In contrast to conditions (d)–(f), which will be understood in part 2 as all pertaining to certain preferred *intensional* relations that Aristotle insists must hold between the terms of legitimate demonstrative premises, the immediacy condition is a purely extensional one entailed more or less straightforwardly by Aristotle's insistence at *Posterior Analytics* 1.14.79a18–32 that syllogistic demonstration must proceed exclusively in the first-figure moods, and more particularly (given that he also requires demonstrative premises to be universal[20]) in Barbara or Celarent.[21] In both of these moods the middle term is included in the major, and either includes the minor (in Barbara) or excludes it (in Celarent), from which it follows within Aristotle's foundational syllogistic scheme that any primary (that is, ultimate and indemonstrable) premise will express an immediate (that is, unmiddled) inclusion or exclusion relation between its terms.[22]

In order to see exactly how what I am calling Aristotelian division constitutes a method for collecting premises that satisfy the immediacy requirement of 71b22, we must take a close look at the safeguards that

Aristotle insists at *Posterior Analytics* 2.13.97a23–26 must be observed if the method is to accomplish its purpose. I have already argued that the establishment of the first of these, that the procedure must (1) confine itself to *essential* (or at least, nonaccidental) connections between terms, should not be understood as something that the method itself is supposed to achieve, but rather as a prior achievement that is presupposed by the possibility of the method's successful operation. In contrast to this, as the method is described in *Posterior Analytics* 2.13 and *Prior Analytics* 1.27–32, it does contain within itself the means to secure the remaining two safeguards mentioned at 97a23–26, namely that the competent divider (2) must take the differentiae in the right order, and (3) must be sure that nothing is left out, and that the securing of these two conditions entails that Aristotelian division constitutes an effective procedure for finding syllogistic premises that express the immediate connections among the terms within a given genus.

Aristotle's recommendation for securing condition (2) is given in an extremely compact and elegant passage in *Posterior Analytics* 2.13: "The order will be [correct] if the first [differentiae] is taken. This will be the one which follows from all of the others, but which they do not follow (for necessarily there will be one such[23]). And when we have taken this away, at once the same procedure [is applied] to the lower terms, for the second will be first among the rest, and the third [will be first] among those that come after [the second]. For when the highest is removed, the next in order of the others will be the first, and similarly for the rest" (97a28–35).

The central idea here is quite straightforward. Supposing that one begins with a set of essential terms within a single genus, Aristotle argues that it is possible to place them in the correct order of inclusion by first finding the one that is nonreciprocally entailed by all the others (which will presumably be the genus itself), next finding the one that is nonreciprocally entailed by all others among the remainder, and continuing in this way until the original set of terms has been exhausted. Even the procedure described here begins to display the characteristic top-to-bottom look of a Platonic Division, but notice that Aristotle is working at this point with an extremely simplistic case involving only a single nonbranching sequence of nested terms.

Nonetheless, it is possible to complicate his procedure in a more realistic direction while still preserving its central idea. We now suppose that we are presented with a set of terms within a single genus which are interrelated by both inclusion and exclusion relations (so that the genus as a whole has a branching structure). Now, as before, we first look for and find the term, A, that is nonreciprocally entailed by all the others (which again is the genus itself). However, when we now look for a single term among the remainder that is nonreciprocally entailed by all of the others, what we find instead is that there are in fact two (or perhaps more) terms, B and C, each of which is nonreciprocally entailed by a certain family of terms within A, which is to say that B and C represent branching nodes of A. Moreover, the same sort of circumstance can recur if we try to find within the family of terms that nonreciprocally entail B, a single term that is nonreciprocally entailed by all of the others: we might very well discover that in fact there are two or more independent families within B's extension, so that B itself is discovered to have a branching structure. And so the method would proceed until the original collection of terms is exhausted.

With this complication installed, Aristotle's procedure for placing the terms of a genus in correct order begins to look even more like a Platonic Division, since it is now seen to involve a descent through the *branching* structure of a given genus, a descent which would presumably culminate at its *infimae* species. But as it now stands, the procedure involves no way to ensure that any or all of the connections uncovered in this descent will be "immediate" in the sense of 71b22. For there is nothing as yet to rule out the case where B nonreciprocally entails A, but only because it non-reciprocally entails some third term, D, that itself nonreciprocally entails A. And by the same token, the entailment relations linking D to both A and B might themselves involve any (finite[24]) number of further inter-mediate terms.

The fundamental difficulty that gives rise to this sort of case, accord-ing to Aristotle's own diagnosis at 96b35−7, is that the original collec-tion of terms subjected to the ordering procedure described at 97a28−35 could not in the first place have contained all of the essence-differentiating terms within the genus under division. (Clearly, in the schematic case just described, if D *had* been included, it would have turned up before B in the ordering procedure.) Consequently, he moves to block this possibility by building into the version of division he is advocating a way of ensuring the third of the safeguards mentioned at 97a23−26, namely that "noth-ing be left out" (μηδὲν παραβάνειν) of the division, as he puts it in a number of places (for example, *Prior Analytics* 1.30.46a25, *Posterior Analytics* 2.5.91b31; 2.13.96b36). Notice that in the branching case de-scribed above, where term A has been discovered to be nonreciprocally entailed by two independent terms, B and C, the problem before us is that these terms may each entail A only through the mediation of other terms (or series of terms) that did not appear in the original collection. At *Posterior Analytics* 96b37–97a6, Aristotle actually describes such a case and provides a way of detecting and correcting its deficiency:

> For when the primary genus is taken, if one of the divisions lower [than the immediate one] is then taken, everything [in the genus] will not fall into this. For instance, not every animal is either whole-winged or split-winged, but every winged animal is, for it is the differentia of *this*. The primary differentiation of animal is that into which all animal falls. And similarly for each of the other divisions, both those outside [a given genus], and those below it. For instance, of bird, that into which all bird falls, and of fish, that into which all fish falls. If you proceed thusly, you will know that nothing has been left out; otherwise things necessarily will be left out without [your] knowing so.

In the example described here, we can let A represent the genus *animal,* and B and C the independent (and indeed mutually exclusive) terms, *whole-winged* and *split-winged,* which presumably are the first remaining terms of the original collection found to entail A nonreciprocally during the procedure for correct ordering described above. The central insight behind the test given in this passage for detecting omissions is contained in the fact that, because that procedure was presumed to operate only on the essence-signifying terms within the genus, which is to say terms denoting differentiae or species, then (assuming that B and C are on the same divisional level) we know that they must either (1) represent a pair of differentiae (or species[25]) that together effect an immediate division of A itself, or (2) represent differentiae of some subdivision D of A, which may be either immediate or mediated by some finite series of divisions. These two general possibilities can be represented schematically as follows:

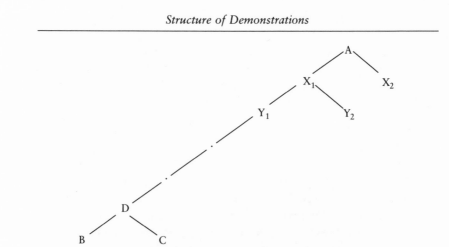

The test employed in the quoted passage, then, effectively separates these possibilities, for only in the first case is it true not only that B and C individually entail A, but also that A entails their disjunction, or in other words, that they are jointly exhaustive of A. Thus, Aristotle argues that even though *whole-winged* and *split-winged* each entail *animal,* and so come *somewhere* after it in the correct ordering of terms, they cannot be *next* in order to A, since (due to the existence of wingless animals) it is not true that every animal is either one or the other. Furthermore, a second look at *Posterior Analytics* 96b37–97a6 shows that what Aristotle is proposing there is not just a method for detecting omissions in the proper ordering of terms, but also one for correcting omissions once found. Suppose it has been discovered according to the above procedure that B and C do not jointly exhaust A, and thus that there must be missing terms between them and it. Aristotle's discussion suggests that one can set about finding those missing terms in the spirit of his program by now trying to find a term (call it D) not appearing in the original collection that is entailed both by B and C, and in turn entails A. In Aristotle's example, the term meeting these conditions is *winged.* Now that we know D is one of the omitted terms between A and B and C, but not necessarily the only one, we can reapply the test for omissions given at 96b37–97a6 at two levels: first by ascertaining whether D is itself jointly exhausted by B and C (if not, there must be missing terms between it and them), and next by first identifying D's codifferentia,[26] E (in Aristotle's, example, *wingless*), and then determining whether D and E jointly exhaust A. If further omissions are discovered during either process, missing terms are added as before, and new tests for omissions are administered. So the process continues until, after some finite number of steps,[27] a complete correct ordering of the terms within A is generated.

To sum up, I have been arguing that because the Aristotelian version of division advocated in *Posterior Analytics* 2.13 and *Prior Analytics* 1.27–32 contains within itself procedures for obtaining a correct and complete ordering of terms (and because it is restricted to terms that signify essence), it is reasonable to view the method as a whole as one by which it is possible to set out all of the immediate essential connections among the terms within a genus, and in that way to systematize the genus prior to construction of syllogistic demonstrations pertinent to its contents. This, I take it, is the rationale for Aristotle's remark at *Posterior Analytics* 2.13.96b15 that division of a genus into atomic kinds is necessary when one is "making a study" (πραγματεύηται) of that genus. However, we have not yet seen how this method figures in Aristotle's views about how one should go about actually collecting the syllogistic premises of demonstrations relevant to the genus under study.

This final connection is made in *Prior Analytics* 1.27, and *Posterior Analytics* 2.14, both of which are best understood as assuming that the prospective demonstrator has already employed Aristotelian division to chart all of the immediate connections within the genus of interest. At *Prior Analytics* 1.27.43b1–5, Aristotle says that in order to collect appropriate premises pertinent to a given subject, it is necessary, after first setting down the subject itself, its definition, and its peculiar properties (that is, all terms that are nonaccidentally coextensional with the subject[28]), to proceed to identify the terms entailed by the subject, the terms that the subject entails, and the terms that are excluded by (and therefore exclude) the subject. Then, at the opening of *Prior Analytics* 1.28, he makes it clear how, on the assumption that this has been done for all of the terms within a genus, it will be possible to obtain the premises necessary to construct a demonstration (in Barbara) of a universal affirmative, "When we wish to establish that some predicate belongs to some whole [that is, to all of some subject], we must look at all the subjects of which the predicate we are establishing is said [that is, the terms which entail the predicate], and the terms which are entailed by the subject, for if there is something the same in these [two groups], the predicate will necessarily belong to the subject" (43b39–44).

There are two ways to understand Aristotle's instruction to examine the terms entailed by the subject and the terms that entail the predicate of the universal affirmative one is trying to demonstrate. He could be thinking here of the field of terms in question prior to the ordering procedures just discussed, in which case the relatively weak point of the passage would certainly hold: if it is known that there is a term, B, that both entails A and is entailed by C, then simple transitivity requires that C entails A. Notice that this tells us there is some syllogistic proof of "All C is A" containing only immediate universal affirmatives as premises, but it provides no way of identifying those premises. If, however, this passage is to be understood as a pertinent part of the discussion begun in *Prior Analytics* 1.27 about how we can actually find the materials for syllogisms (43a20–21), the method by which we can apprehend the starting points (or ultimate premises[29]) concerning each syllogistic problem (a21–22), and our ability to construct syllogisms (a24), then it is more reasonable to suppose that the field of terms involved has already been arranged by an Aristotelian division into the correct and complete ordering. On this supposition, Aristotle's point is now a stronger and more helpful one—if in the concurrent processes of tracing A's descendants and C's ancestors through this ordering, one happens upon the same term (B) from both directions:

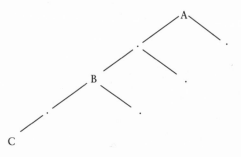

then one has thereby not only discovered that there must be a syllogistic demonstration of "All C is A," but also connected A and C through a series of immediate entailment relations, and in this way actually collected all of immediate (universal affirmative) premises of the syllogisms in Barbara needed to construct that demonstration. Aristotle makes a restricted version of the same point in *Posterior Analytics* 2.14, after using language very similar to that of 97a28–35 in Chapter 13 to advocate once more his own version of division: "For example, if the genus *animal* is what we should study, [we should discover] what belongs to all animals. Having grasped these, [we must identify] what follows upon all of the first of the remainder (e.g. if this is bird, what follows from all bird), and proceed thusly, always taking the 'nearest' (ἐγγύτατα) [division]" (98a4–7). Aristotle then explains how this point can prove useful in demonstrating that certain attributes belong to certain subjects: "Let A stand for *animal*, B for the attributes belonging to every animal, and C, D, and E for the sorts of animal. Now it is clear on account of what B belongs to D: on account of A. And likewise for the others [i.e., for C and E]; and the same reasoning always applies to the terms lower [than C, D and E]" (94a7–12). Here again the point is that, since we have already discovered that B is one of the (nonaccidental) attributes belonging immediately to *animal* and that D is an immediate subdivision of A (in other words, that both "All A is B" and "All D is A" are true and immediate), we are in position to construct a single-syllogism demonstration in Barbara of "All D is B."

The same sort of interpretation can also be given to the parallel point Aristotle makes at *Prior Analytics* 44a1–7 for the case where one wants to prove a universal negative: "Whenever it is required [to show] that some predicate belongs to none of some subject, it is necessary to consider the terms which are entailed by the subject, and those which cannot belong to the predicate . . . for if any of these is the same the predicate cannot belong to any of the subject." Let us suppose that the universal negative to be proved in this case is "No C is A." Aristotle's point is that if one were to discover in the correct and complete ordering given by Aristotelian division a term B that is an ancestor of C and immediately excludes either A or some ancestor of A, or schematically, that the following ordering obtains:

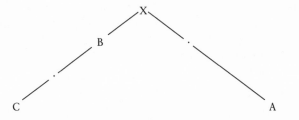

then one would possess all the immediate universal premises (one negative, and the rest affirmative) needed to complete a syllogistic demonstration of "No C is A" (in Barbara and Celarent[30]).

I have been arguing that when Aristotelian division is carried into the specialized contexts of *Posterior Analytics* where Aristotle is concerned specifically with the construction of demonstrative syllogisms, it becomes in effect an absolutely necessary and integral presyllogistic stage in the overall process of generating scientific knowledge. It is, moreover, this *framing stage* of demonstration that proves to be the locus of operations for the various types of ἀρχαί and λαμβανόμενα catalogued in *Posterior Analytics* 1.10. If this two-stage interpretation of demonstration is correct, then it should be possible to understand each type of ἀρχαί in terms of the structural features of the framing stage and its place in the overall theory of demonstration. The most important of these types, the ὅροι discussed at length in Chapters 3 to 10 of Book 2, will be seen in the next chapter to lie at the very heart of the framing procedure. But first, three other types (*generic existence assumptions, generic meaning assumptions,* and the "logical" *common axioms* of Noncontradiction and Excluded Middle) will be interpreted in the remainder of this chapter as constituting various background assumptions necessary for the completion of the framing procedure prior to the actual construction of syllogistic demonstrations.

THE BACKGROUND ASSUMPTIONS OF DEMONSTRATION

A good place to start this procedure is with one of the most widely discussed and least understood passages in the entire *Posterior Analytics*. Speaking of the limitations his theory places on what must be proved and what can be assumed by a science, Aristotle issues the following seemingly enigmatic remark: "Proper (ἴδια) to each science are the subjects whose existence it assumes, and whose per se attributes (ὑπάρχοντα καθ'αὑτά) it studies. . . . Of the subjects both the existence (τὸ εἶναι) and the meaning (τοδὶ εἶναι) are assumed, but as for the per se attributes, only the meaning (τί σημαίνει) is assumed" (1.10.76b5–7).

It will be convenient to dissect this complex assertion (which echoes 76a31–7 and is itself echoed by 76b12–16) into four discrete principles of restriction, which can then be discussed separately.

> (R1) Every science must assume the existence of its subject-genus.[31]
>
> (R2) Every science must assume the meaning of its subject-genus.
>
> (R3) Every science must assume the meaning of the per se attributes of its subject-genus.
>
> (R4) Every science must prove the existence of the per se attributes of its subject-genus.

Of the various items mentioned in these principles, the *meaning assumptions* mentioned in (R3) will turn out to be the most important, since they will be seen to provide the substantive content of Aristotelian ἀπόδειξις. In chapter 2 we shall consider exactly how these substantive meaning assumptions fit into the foundational structure of demonstration, and in part 2 we shall go on to explore the precise nature of the per se connections conveyed by these assumptions. For the moment, however, our concern is to determine the import of Aristotle's assertion of (R1) at 76b5–7, that every science must assume the "existence" (τὸ εἶναι) of the genus it studies. Jaakko Hintikka, who is inclined toward strict syllogisticism, characteristically understands the immediate exegetical question posed by this restriction in a way that leads him to employ an interpretational device that is at once implausible and unnecessary. In keeping with his general commitment to interpret all ἀρχαί and λαμβανόμενα as syllogistic "premises" (προτάσεις), he presumes that the "assumptions of existence" discussed here must constitute a certain kind of predication that can both serve as ultimate syllogistic premises, and at the same time ensure existential import for the widest term of a science (which import, in Hintikka's words, is then "carried downwards from wider terms to narrower ones in a sequence of scientific syllogisms").[32] But finding nothing in Aristotle's texts that explicitly meets these specifications, Hintikka is forced to supply referents for (R1) on Aristotle's behalf. As a result, he finally identifies these assumptions of existence as a peculiar sort of "first premise" that is also a "kind of definition (ὅρος) [of the] widest term of a given science."[33] They are, in other words, premises that define the subject-genera of their respective sciences. Thus, where G is the genus of the science S_G, and Def(G) is the definition of G, Hintikka's proposal is that

(1) All Gs are Def(G)s

is to be found among the ultimate premises of the syllogistic demonstrations within S_G. In addition, he contends that these topmost premises are understood by Aristotle to entail universal existence claims, in this case,

(2) All Gs exist.

Finally, in Hintikka's view, the existential force of (1) represented by this implication is then "percolated down" to the ultimate demonstrata of the justificatory chains in which (1) functions as an ultimate premise.

The most serious problem with this attempt to identify and explicate the existence assumptions in principle (R1) as generic (that is, topmost), immediate syllogistic premises is quite simply that Hintikka's account of the latter is internally inconsistent. For in the schematic illustration above, G is, *ex hypothesi,* the widest term in S_G. Now (1), as an immediate premise that defines G, must presumably do so at least partly by connecting it with its immediate taxonomic superior. But if this is so, it follows that (1) contains a term wider than G, and so cannot (contrary to what Hintikka claims) function as a topmost premise (or in any other capacity) within S_G.

There is some reason to believe that Hintikka is sensitive to this difficulty, since he apparently hedges on his claim that (1) defines G with the following qualification, saying, "Yet these (premises) have the peculiarity that they do not contribute very much to specifying all the different elements that would go into a full definition (of the essence) of the genus,"[34] and this would certainly have the effect of blocking the inference just rehearsed that (1) contains a term wider than G.

However, even if it is allowed that this does not amount to a simple retraction of his earlier claim that (1) *defines* G, this maneuver still offers no hope of salvation for Hintikka's account. For as he recognizes, denying (1) the status of a full-fledged definition makes it "easily appear . . . (as) not a substantial assumption at all, but rather a *mere definitory reformulation of a tautology* of the form (3) Every G is a G."[35] But even supposing that we grant this dubious distinction between definitions and "mere definitory reformulations," Hintikka's "topmost" premises still cannot do the work he has in mind for them. To begin with, nowhere in the *Analytics* do we find syllogistic examples (scientific or otherwise) containing such tautological premises. And even worse (for Hintikka's account), Aristotle shows himself on a number of occasions to be fully aware of the *grammatical* possibility of formulae like (3), and he plainly does not regard such logical monstrosities as legitimate instances of predication, much less as acceptable premises in scientific syllogisms.[36]

It is important to keep in mind that these problems are not properly Aristotle's; they arise only in the attempt to interpret his (R1) in accordance with strict syllogisticism. Once the unnecessarily rigid requirements of that program are abandoned, however, the meaning of (R1) becomes both intelligible and unproblematic. The method of Aristotelian division, as I am interpreting it, is to be understood in the first instance as a procedure involving the definitions of *things* (or *kinds* of things) rather than words. As such, it is to be sharply distinguished from the activities of the lexicographer, who is concerned to chart relations among linguistic entities without paying much attention to the things these entities are supposed to denote.[37] Hence, unlike that other sort of investigation, Aristotle's method is premised upon, and initiated by, confrontation with, or contemplation of, a group of things that actually exist, or are at least supposed to exist, which one is interested in dividing up into its smallest natural classifications.[38] Any application of the method, therefore, will naturally involve the presupposition that the genus being divided actually does exist (that is, is a genus of real things). Indeed, this much is acknowledged explicitly by Aristotle in *Posterior Analytics* 2.10, when he comments that unless it is known that a thing exists, any proposed definition of it (even if formally correct) will fall short of stating the thing's "essence" (τί ἐστι), and must instead be thought of as nothing more than an "account of the meaning of the word" (λόγος τοῦ τί σημαίνει τὸ ὄνομα).[39] Now if I am right that what I have described as Aristotelian division is an essential first stage of demonstration, the rationale for (R1) becomes apparent. It is simply Aristotle's formal recognition that the very nature of this presyllogistic procedure requires that it cannot be performed (and so demonstrative premises cannot be collected) without the prior assumption that the contents of the subject-genus actually exist to be divided.

Notice that a parallel rationale can be given for (R2), which, it will be recalled, states that a science must also "assume the meaning of its subject-genus." As was just seen in the criticism of Hintikka's interpretation of (R1), this cannot mean that the ultimate demonstrative premises of a science must include the definition of its subject-genus. But here again, the difficulty can be circumvented by means of the simple insight that (R2) also pertains not to the actual construction of demonstrative syllogisms, but to the divisional procedure that necessarily precedes it. For in addition to knowing (or supposing) that there is in fact a genus of things to be divided, it would also seem to be necessary, before a διαίρεσις can proceed, to possess some minimal background information about how the genus itself fits into the wider scheme of things. Imagine, for example, the futility of trying to divide up the land animals in ignorance of the fact that they are a sort of animal.[40] At the very least, there would seem to be no way to rule out such far-fetched offerings as flytraps, or even statues, as counterexamples to proposed classifications based on diet or means of support. This commonsense requirement, that one must know (in some sense) what one is dividing in order to divide it, is one that could hardly escape Aristotle's notice, and it is just this, I believe, that he means to express by (R2).

Once these two preconditions have been secured, the framing stage of demonstration then proceeds along the lines set out above. Beginning at the top, one moves downward through the genus by specifying finer and finer sets of differentiae, taking care that the differentiae are taken in the right order, and that at each level one takes the immediate, or "proper," differentiae of the kind being subdivided.[41] The epistemological effect of this process is critical to the operation of Aristotelian science: whereas prior to the framing procedure a given subject-genus might (for all that is known) be no more than a mere aggregatory grouping with no interesting internal structure, afterwards it is revealed to be a hierarchy whose constituent necessary, immediate connections are expressed by (and so give rise to) the ultimate atomic premises of the demonstrative syllogism-chains within the science which studies that genus.

Finally, the postulation of a presyllogistic framing stage provides a way of understanding how the "logical" axioms[42] of Noncontradiction and Excluded Middle figure in demonstration, without casting them in the unlikely role of syllogistic premises.[43] For within that framework, both of these ἀρχαί are naturally presupposed by the systematization of a genus into a hierarchy of the sort Aristotle envisions. This hardly needs showing in the case of Noncontradiction; clearly no coherent classificatory scheme whatever will be possible if it is allowed that one and the same item can be simultaneously included and excluded by another. This point is recognized by Aristotle at *Metaphysics* 4.4.1007a21−36, where (apparently relying on *Categories* 5.3b25−33) he argues that to say A is both B and not B is in effect to make B an accident of A. Therefore, he reasons, to deny Noncontradiction is to do away with the essential/accidental distinction, and thus to rule out the possibility of delineating essential kinds by means of division or any other method.

The case for Excluded Middle, while not quite so obvious, is evidently just as compelling for Aristotle, for he sees the principle as required to secure the requirement discussed earlier that the division "leave nothing out." For suppose that in the attempt to subdivide A, we succeed in discovering two (or more) differentiae, B and C, which are known to entail A and to exclude each other. Still, even if we knew that B and not-C were equivalent, it could not be inferred from this that B and C *exhausted* A (that is, that all non-Cs in A were Bs) except by invoking Excluded Middle to assume that every A *either has or lacks* C. As a matter of fact, this is the form of an inference Aristotle himself performs at *Posterior Analytics* 1.4.73b22–4, concerning the per se attributes *odd* and *even* and their logical relations to the genus of numbers.[44]

Of course, such formal principles as have been discussed so far are sufficient to determine only the broad schematic structure of an Aristotelian demonstrative science. In any particular case this schema will have to be filled in by a set of substantive principles that provide the actual content of the explanations constructed within the science in question, and this is presumably the function of what are referred to as meaning assumptions in (R3). The next order of business, then, is to develop some understanding of the role these meaning assumptions play in the theory of demonstration.

TWO

———

Demonstration and Definition

I suggested at the beginning of chapter 1 that the opening statement of the *Posterior Analytics*, that all discursive knowledge must come out of pre-existent knowledge, is a deliberate allusion to the paradox of learning formulated by Plato in the *Meno*. What is more, this Platonic theme is sustained and developed throughout *Posterior Analytics* 1.1 and then resonates throughout the remainder of the treatise. In a manner again strikingly reminiscent of the *Meno*, Aristotle introduces at 71a17–29 a distinction between two ways of knowing a general proposition: (1) the "unqualified" (ἁπλῶς) way (which I shall designate *de re*), which entails knowledge of its application to all the particulars that happen to fall under its terms; and (2) a "merely universal" way, which does not entail such knowledge of its particular instantiations.[1] He then goes on at a29–30 to tout this distinction between de re and merely universal knowledge as just what is needed to resolve the paradox of the *Meno*.

It is remotely possible that the purpose of this passage is dramatic rather than systematic: that because the work to follow is, after all, about a certain kind of knowledge, Aristotle desires to warm his audience to his subject by trotting out a familiar old puzzle about the general subject of knowledge, which is then dropped for good when it has had its salutatory effect. Such easy answers to questions about Aristotle's expository practices are always possible (if never very satisfying), especially when the work in question has a reputation for being "tentative and unpolished,"[2] but in this case the suggestion lacks plausibility. For at 71a12–17, the passage directly preceding the initial appearance of the distinction between de re and merely universal knowledge, Aristotle offers yet another epistemological distinction, between two subkinds of preexistent knowledge—knowledge of facts (existential facts in particular), and knowledge of meanings—and there is no question that the latter distinction eventually comes to occupy a prominent place in the theory of demonstrative knowledge presented in the *Posterior Analytics*.[3] We are thus naturally encouraged to expect that the distinction between de re and merely universal knowledge likewise will eventually have important work to do in Aristotle's theory.

One of my chief aims in this chapter will be to show that in fact this distinction pervades nearly all of the important doctrines of the *Posterior Analytics*. More particularly, I shall argue that appreciating its centrality to the treatise provides the key insights necessary both to understanding the logical character of the substantive meaning assumptions referred to at *Posterior Analytics* 76b5–7 and to seeing exactly how they function in Aristotle's theory of demonstration. Furthermore, I shall argue that this distinction is also crucial to Aristotle's subtle and complex final position in *Posterior Analytics* 2.3–10 on the question of the exact relationship between demonstration and definition.

THE MEANING ASSUMPTIONS OF DEMONSTRATION

Let's now turn to yet another of the metascientific principles introduced in chapter 1:

> (R3) Every science must assume the meaning of the per
> se (καθ'αὑτό) attributes of its subject-genus. (*Pos-*
> *terior Analytics* 1.10.76b5)

The central work of part 2 will be to explore the various sorts of non-accidental connections Aristotle means to include here under the heading *per se,* and his various motivations for doing so, but now we want to focus on how the assumptions mentioned in (R3) function in the overall process of demonstration. Besides this passage, there are many others (for example *Posterior Analytics* 1.10.76a32–37, b6–11, b15) which express this restriction, and still others which indicate (what evidently comes to the same thing) that "definitions" (ὅροι) are among the "first principles" (ἀρχαί) of demonstration (*Posterior Analytics* 1.2.72a15–25; 1.10.76b35–38). According to the central tenet of strict syllogisticism, we are to understand Aristotle to be saying here that definitions are among the ultimate *syllogistic premises* of demonstration. With respect to syntax, this poses no problem, since much of what Aristotle says about definitions throughout the *Organon* makes it very easy to think of them as having at least the form of simple universal affirmative sentences.[4] Indeed, this much is virtually explicit at *Posterior Analytics* 2.13.97b26. However, as soon as questions are raised about Aristotle's intended semantic interpretation of ὅροι, and more specifically about their existential import, their credentials as appropriate syllogistic material at once become suspect. At *Posterior Analytics* 1.10.76b35–77a5, definitions are explicitly ruled out as "premises" (προτάσεις) on the grounds that they "make no assertions of existence or non-existence" (οὐδὲν γὰρ εἶναι ἢ μὴ εἶναι λέγεται; b35), which is to say that they lack existential force.[5] Moreover, any doubt that this exclusion is based on the general theory of the syllogism, and not on any special constraints on the premises of demonstrative syllogisms, is removed by *Posterior Analytics* 1.2.72a8–25, which makes the reasons behind the exclusion altogether transparent. There Aristotle first recalls his insistence at *Prior Analytics* 1.1.24a17 that every syllogistic premise must be either an "affirmation" (λόγος καταφατικός) or a "denial" (λόγος ἀποφατικός), or as he puts it at *Posterior Analytics* 1.2.72a9, "one or the other part of a proposition" (ἀπόφανσις), and then proceeds immediately (at 72a20–1) to state as a corollary to this that legitimate syllogistic premises must, again, assert that "something does or does not exist."[6]

To the strict syllogisticist, who is committed to holding that all ἀρχαί are demonstrative premises, this presents the enormous difficulty of showing that ὅροι do after all have a rightful place among the premises of syllogistic demonstration, despite all the passages just mentioned which seem to deny them just that. Hintikka attempts to get around this difficulty by pointing to Aristotle's well-documented tendency to equivocate in his own key philosophical terminology. He argues in effect that the term ὅρος takes on an extraordinarily narrow sense in *Posterior Analytics* 1.2 and 1.10 that picks out only so-called "nominal definitions" (λόγοι τοῦ τί σημαίνει τὰ ὀνόματα),[7] which do indeed lack existential import, and that the above passages therefore need not be interpreted as ruling out *all* definitions as premises, but only this special subclass of them. By contrast, according to Hintikka, there are other passages in the

Posterior Analytics (especially 1.22.83b32–84a6) that indicate there is at least one other sort of definition—namely those formulae, called ἄτομοι at 2.5.91b32, which express immediate connections between terms— which *do* have existential force, and so can function as premises in syllogistic demonstrations.[8]

It is hard to see how Hintikka's strict syllogisticism can be compatible with his position that there are some Aristotelian definitions that *cannot* function as demonstrative premises. Nonetheless, I believe he is quite right to argue that Aristotle does sharply distinguish between the ὅροι of *Posterior Analytics* 1.2 and 10, and the "immediate" ultimate demonstrative premises of *Posterior Analytics* 1.22 and 2.5, and moreover that he does so precisely on the grounds that only the latter have existential force. As a matter of fact, a closer look at what I have called the framing stage of demonstration provides a very plausible explanation of why this distinction should be so important to Aristotle.

It was argued in chapter 1 that the Aristotelian adaptation of Platonic Division involves, not the discovery of definitions, but the deployment of a set of previously apprehended "definitional assumptions" (ὅροι) upon some field of inquiry. That is, I argued that where Plato conceives ὅροι as the ultimate products of his preferred epistemological method, for Aristotle they are mere starting points—part of the preexistent material out of which knowledge *simpliciter* is ultimately generated. I now want to pursue the question of what it is about the logical character of definitions that motivates Aristotle to assign them this merely contributory role in his theory of demonstrative knowledge.

REFERENTIAL AND PLATONISTIC UNIVERSALS

It will be helpful at this point to notice an important respect in which Aristotle's proposed solution to Meno's paradox in *Posterior Analytics* 1.1 mimics the structure of the solution put forward by Plato himself at *Meno* 85D–E and developed through his middle dialogues. Both solutions depend on separating two forms of knowledge (or apparent knowledge), one of which is of universals (in Plato's case, of the Forms) and the other of particulars. But this structural parallel notwithstanding, the fundamental epistemological positions from which the two proposals issue are diametrically opposed. For Plato it is *universal* knowledge (of Forms) that turns out to be not just the highest but the only form of genuine knowledge, while so-called knowledge of mundane participants in Forms is eventually consigned at *Republic* 5.477–78 to the category of mere "belief" (δόξα) or "opinion" (πίστις). On the other hand, Aristotle, true to his anti-Platonic metaphysical proclivities, makes precisely the reverse assignments of relative value to these two sorts of cognitive state. It is what I have called "de re" knowledge—the sort that entails knowledge of particular cases—that is said in *Posterior Analytics* 1.1 to be knowledge in the "strict" or "unqualified" (ἁπλῶς) sense, whereas the type whose objects are universals is described as knowledge only in a qualified sense (71a26–29).

Before proceeding further, we should try to get a more precise understanding of Aristotle's characterization of de re knowledge at 71a17–19 as "knowledge of what was known previously, and at the same time . . . of the things which happen to fall under the universal of which there is knowledge." One possible construction of this description is anticipated and explicitly ruled out by Aristotle himself at 71a30–b3. In that passage he argues against the suggestion that the objects of de re knowledge of the truth of

(1) Every pair is even

are limited to those individual instances that are known by the subject to be pairs, so that to say that *a* knows de re that every pair is even is just to say that everything known by *a* to be a pair is also known by *a* to be even. The problem with this construction, as Aristotle quite correctly deduces, is that it improperly restricts the subject matter of (1) itself only to pairs whose existence has been apprehended by *a*, whereas the proper scope of the sentence, and therefore of *a*'s de re knowledge of its truth (as Aristotle puts it) is all pairs that have been *proved* to be even. These he insists are not limited to pairs known by *a*, but include all pairs without qualification. Put positively and in the language of recent discussions of propositional attitudes, Aristotle's point is that de re knowledge contexts are transparent in the sense that if *a* knows de re that (1) is true, then it follows that for every pair *b*, *a* knows that *b* is even, whether or not *a* knows of *b*'s existence.

In his notes to this passage, Jonathan Barnes has tried to capture this feature by giving the following analysis of *a*'s having de re knowledge of (1):

If anything is a pair, then *a* knows that it is even.[9]

This is very nearly correct, since it would in every case warrant the inference from "*b* is a pair" to "*a* knows *b* is even." However, this universally quantified formulation, unlike its Aristotelian counterpart, does not make reference to all the actual pairs there are, and so does not involve presuppositions of their existence. Hence, it could be (vacuously) true even if no pairs existed.[10] For this reason, I think it is better to represent the transparency of de re knowledge by using a more Aristotelian form of sentence to be discussed shortly:

> Every (actual) pair is known by *a* to be even,

which entails Barnes's analysis but at the same time is intended to carry such existential presuppositions.

True to the general quasi-epistemological motif of the *Posterior Analytics* described in my introduction, Aristotle's proposed treatment of the *Meno* paradox is based on an epistemological distinction between two types of knowledge, or more accurately, between two ways of knowing the truth of single universal sentences such as

> (2) Every man is animal.

Indeed, I have suggested that this serves to underscore the fact that he sees his solution to the paradox as a direct and opposed response to Plato's own. Nevertheless, it is possible to see behind this epistemological distinction a parallel semantic distinction between two very different ways of understanding the logical character of (2) itself. On one hand, we could understand it as a sentence about every single individual falling under its subject term, that is, about every actually existent man,[11] so that its truth would entail a conjunction of singular propositions.[12] On this construction, the subject term of a universal sentence makes (distributed) reference to every one of its actual instances, and so, by virtue of this referential function, the sentence as a whole involves a presupposition of the *singular* existence of each of those individuals.

Here it is important to see that one cannot capture the existential force of (2) in modern predicate calculus by simply conjoining a universally quantified version of it with an existentially quantified statement bestowing general existence on its subject:

> (2′) If anything is a man, it is an animal, and there are
> men.

As with all attempts to translate between the Aristotelian and Post-Fregean logics for general terms, this fails to respect a fundamental difference between the ways in which they deal with existence. In the logic of quantifiers, existential import is always conveyed by means of existentially quantified statements of *general* existence (that is, nonemptiness of predicate extensions),[13] such as "There are men." On the other hand, in Aristotelian logic it is always carried by *singular* existential presuppositions generated by the fundamental idea that general subjects like "Every man," no less than singular subjects like "Socrates," actually make reference to the individuals to which they apply.[14] One way to see this difference is to notice that if the membership of the human species were (partly or wholly) different from what it actually is, then the facts expressed by (2) would differ accordingly; that is, the sentence would be about a different group of individuals. By contrast, the propositions expressed by (2') would remain unaltered in such a case.[15] In order to represent this distinctive feature of Aristotelian logic, I shall hereafter refer to universal sentences under this interpretation as *referential universals*.

Alternatively, sentence (2) could also be understood as making no reference whatever to concrete individuals, but instead as expressing a (necessary) relation between the universal kinds signified by its subject and predicate terms. Viewed in this way, the sentence could be analyzed as the second-order statement that the human species is a species of animal.[16] For reasons that I hope are obvious I shall call universal sentences under this second style of interpretation *Platonistic*. With this distinction in place, then, it is possible to understand the epistemological moral Aristotle claims in *Posterior Analytics* 1.1 to draw from his treatment of Meno's Paradox as the conclusion that universal statements capable of conveying the highest form of knowledge (demonstrative knowledge) must be referential, whereas the preexistent substantive meaning assumptions from which this knowledge is generated are conveyed by Platonistic universal statements. This then leaves two questions outstanding: how does Aristotle think these Platonistic definitions are acquired in the first place, and why does he relegate them to this inferior position?

THE ACQUISITION OF DEFINITIONS

One particularly elegant feature of the overall design of the *Posterior Analytics* is that its very last chapter (Book 2, Chapter 19) returns to the thought with which the treatise opens, namely that knowledge based on reasoned justification must be generated out of preexistent knowledge of its foundations. We have seen that this Platonically inspired idea is reflected in Aristotle's theory by the requirement that any demonstrative science must take as given a distinctive set of "starting points" (ἀρχαί) that are used in the framing stage of demonstration to generate the most basic premises out of which syllogistic demonstrations within that science are composed. But this of course does not even touch the residual question of how these initial starting points come to be acquired or justified in the first place.

I should point out to begin with that because the class of Aristotelian ἀρχαί has already been seen to be extremely heterogeneous in its makeup, there is no reason to expect that this question would receive a single, simple answer from Aristotle. And indeed, he appears to recognize very different manners of justification for different sorts of ἀρχαί. In particular, his proposed defense in *Metaphysics* Γ 4 of the so-called common axiom of Noncontradiction (which was classified in chapter 1 as one of the nonsubstantive background assumptions of Aristotelian division needed to generate the premises of demonstrative syllogisms) appears to proceed according to relatively informal dialectical methods of the sort set forth in the *Topics*. On the other hand, he seems to think that another sort of background assumption, those conveying the existence of the objects of demonstration, requires no discursive justification at all, but rather can be secured simply by perceiving the objects in question, or perhaps (in the case of mathematics) even by simply hypothesizing their existence.

But whereas Aristotle's views about the acquisition of these various sorts of nonsubstantive starting points of demonstration themselves remain for the most part in the background of the *Posterior Analytics,* he evidently regards ὅροι—the ultimate meaning assumptions of demonstration—as so central to his theory that he chooses to close the whole treatise with a discussion of how they in particular come to be apprehended prior to the generation of demonstrative knowledge. To be sure, the fact that *Posterior Analytics* 2.19 is concerned specifically with definitional ἀρχαί does not come out clearly in Aristotle's initial formulation at 99b15–19 of the main question to be pursued in the chapter: "Hence, concerning syllogism and demonstration, what each of them is and how it comes about, is now apparent; and likewise concerning demonstrative knowledge, for [the issues] are the same. But [we must now make clear] concerning the starting points (ἀρχῶν), how they come to be recognized (γνώριμοι), and what is the condition (ἕξις[17]) which recognizes them." It is, however, evidenced in his more precise reiteration of the question at b20–25, where he characterizes the "primary starting points" (πρώτας ἀρχάς) whose provenance is at issue as "immediate" (ἀμέσους): "Concerning the recognition (γνῶσιν) of 'immediates,' one might ask (1) whether it's the same [as that of nonimmediates] or not, and (2) whether there is knowledge (ἐπιστήμη) of both, or if knowledge is [only] of [nonimmediates] while [the cognitive ἕξις, which apprehends immediates] is of a different sort."[18]

It is important to recognize that even though neither Plato nor his *Meno* are here mentioned by name, this final chapter of the *Posterior Analytics,* no less than the first, takes the famous paradox about learning formulated in that dialogue as its primary point of departure. This is plain almost from its opening when, in the continuation of the passage just quoted, Aristotle consciously models his proposed approach on the *Meno* paradox by posing the ancillary question of whether the sought-after account of the preexistent apprehension of immediate demonstrative first principles will involve (a) postulating the emergence of entirely new cognitive ἕξεις in the subject's soul, or whether (as in the Platonic doctrine of Recollection) it will instead require (b) the postulation of pre-existent ἕξεις of which the subject is unaware: "[We must inquire] whether cognitive states not [already] in the subject come into being, or whether they had [simply] not been noticed (λεληθασιν)[19] to be within the subject" (99b21–26).

From this point Aristotle proceeds to argue that the seeming exhaustiveness of the disjunction between (a) and (b) sets up an apparent dilemma, but that this dilemma is in fact only apparent. He moves directly against (a) at b28–30 by recalling his conclusion in Book 1, Chapter 1 (which in turn looks back to the *Meno*) that it is not possible for knowledge or learning to arise out of a complete lack of cognition on the subject's part. His rejection of (b), on the other hand, is qualified: he claims at b26–27 that it is absurd (ἄτοπον) to think that one could happen to possess a cognitive ἕξις that is "more accurate" (ἀκριβεστέρας) than demonstration, while remaining ignorant that one possessed it. The qualification here is significant, for it turns out that Aristotle's subsequent proposal for avoiding the dilemma is to deny (a) by holding that there is a certain preexistent ἕξις from which the apprehension of first principles (and a fortiori, all demonstrative knowledge) ultimately arises, while at the same time avoiding the absurd form of (b) by denying that this ἕξις is an *occurrent* cognitive state (in which case, it would presumably have to be more accurate than demonstrative knowledge, and could therefore not be possessed inadvertently). Rather, he maintains, the ἕξις in question is a certain kind of cognitive *capacity,* that is to say, a δύναμις,[20] for acquiring such occurrent states, which is not more accurate than those occurrent states themselves: "However, it is apparent both that one cannot possess such states without knowing so, and also that they could not come to be if one didn't possess any [prior] state at all; therefore, it is necessary for one to have a certain sort of capacity (δύναμις), but one which will not be 'more worthy with respect to accuracy' (τιμιωτέρα κατ' ἀκρίβειαν) than those others" (99b30–34).

The very next sentence makes it seem as if Aristotle goes on to identify this δύναμις with that discerning capacity, present in all animals, called "perception" (αἴσθησις). However, his subsequent account at 99b36–100b5 of the "inductive process" (ἐπαγωγή) through which he thinks one comes to apprehend immediate definitional connections makes it clear that his point is really that basic animal perception is *temporally speaking* the first capacity that must be activated in the apprehension of these connections (so that there is a temporal sense in which the entire process could be said to arise ultimately out of perception), and not the patently absurd notion that animal perception alone comprises the cognitive capacity for grasping immediate definitional first principles.[21] For what emerges out of that account is that this latter capacity is actually a complex of simpler capacities that involves not only perception (which is shared by all animals) but also "memory" (μνήμη), which Aristotle believes only some kinds of animal possess, as well as "intuition" (νοῦς), a very special human capacity for grasping universals in perception,[22] which he believes belongs only to rational animals.[23] Thus, if Aristotle is to be taken literally at 99b35 when he intimates that the ἕξις responsible for apprehension of definitional first principles is the faculty of perception, he must be understood as referring, not to the rudimentary capacity exhibited by animals of any degree of complexity, but rather to a complex "perceptual" capacity special to rational beings—a kind of perception that is peculiarly *human*.[24]

So Aristotle finally answers the opening question of *Posterior Analytics* 2.19 by locating the ἕξις that apprehends the most important ultimate first principles of demonstration in the cluster of capacities belonging universally and especially to humans *qua* rational beings. For this reason the chapter is extremely well placed, and indeed is best thought of as an appendix to the main treatise, since it is not concerned with demonstration proper, but rather with the source of the preexistent cognitive material required to get that justificatory program off the ground. For the "inductive" process it describes is one that could be (and in fact is) performed not just by the Aristotelian scientist, but by virtually any well-developed mature human specimen (or perhaps, as *we* might say, any such that mastered a language with general terms), solely by virtue of having a rational soul, quite independently of whether it had any inclination or ability for the scientific enterprise. In other words, as *Posterior Analytics* 2.19 characterizes the manner in which the definitional first principles of demonstration are initially apprehended, it turns out to be nothing other than the process of general concept formation, which is available to all humans, and which must already have been accomplished before there can be any question of doing Aristotelian science. In the final analysis, it is this peculiarly human, but not peculiarly "scientific," activity that Aristotle sees as providing the preexistent substantive material out of which demonstrative knowledge is ultimately generated.

THE LOGICAL CHARACTER OF DEFINITIONS

The remaining question posed earlier is why Aristotle denies that apprehension of this preexistent material qualifies as knowledge simpliciter. The answer to this lies ultimately in another, related respect besides that discussed in chapter 1, in which the framing stage of Aristotelian demonstration differs importantly from Platonic διαίρεσις. In light of what is known about the metaphysics of Plato's middle period, it would be very hard to deny that for him the ultimate objects of διαίρεσις must be *separated* universals, that is to say, Platonic Forms. Hence, any salient *extensional* relations that are noticed among classes of particulars during the process of division must be understood finally as mundane manifestations of eternal, unchanging, and necessary "interweaving" (συμπλοκή), that is, *intensional,* relations among such Forms,[25] which are the real subject matter of the ὅροι generated by Plato's method. But this means that once such a Platonic definition has been acquired, any or all of the sensible particulars that helped give rise to it might be forgotten (or for that matter destroyed) without diminishing the quality of knowledge of the definition itself one whit. This of course would not be at all troubling to a Platonist, for whom particulars are after all just imperfect and transitory participants in the Forms. On the other hand, it is easy to see why an immanent realist[26] like Aristotle would be quite uncomfortable about the admission of such free-floating universal knowledge that is not necessarily pegged to any concrete individuals. This, I think, is at bottom why his theory of demonstration systematically gives pride of place to de re knowledge of ἄτομοι and is inclined to demote merely universal knowledge of ὅροι to the level of preexistent epistemic material out of which demonstrative knowledge is generated.

DEMONSTRATION AND SYSTEMATICITY

There is, however, a second and equally important reason for Aristotle to deny preexistent knowledge of ὅροι the status of knowledge in his strictest sense of the term, and there is more than a little irony in the fact that this reason also seems to be taken from Plato. On the basis of what has been said so far, nothing in the theory of demonstration rules out the possibility that one could acquire any number of these ἀρχαί and yet not have the slightest idea how they (or any subgroups of them) could be drawn together into some systematic and coherent scheme of scientific explanation. Now it was mentioned earlier that Plato regards definitions generated by his method of division as objects of the highest form of knowledge. Furthermore, in light of certain views evidenced in the *Theaetetus* (the one Platonic dialogue devoted exclusively to epistemological concerns), it is easy enough to understand the reason for this high regard. This dialogue, like so many others, ends in apparent perplexity, but nearly everyone agrees that it makes progress in the direction of establishing that, whatever genuine knowledge should turn out to be, it must somehow involve having "true belief accompanied by a *logos*." The final perplexity of the dialogue then arises because the interlocutors cannot seem to find a defensible understanding of what should count as the right sort of logos. However, Myles Burnyeat and others[27] have argued convincingly that in the closing sections of the work, Plato expresses a definite attraction to (without quite endorsing) what has been called the "interrelational model" of justification, according to which a logos of the right sort makes clear the place which the object of knowledge occupies within a suitably large and systematic field of interrelated objects. It should be apparent, however, how a definition of the sort generated by the Platonic method of division exhibited in the *Sophist* might be thought of in just this way, since it takes the form of a logos that specifies the exact sequence of divisional nodes traversed between the original genus subjected to the division and the bottommost item finally defined by it.[28]

However, as Burnyeat also points out,[29] Aristotle's *Posterior Analytics*, no less than Plato's *Theaetetus*, is firm in its insistence that the title of "knowledge in the unqualified sense," (or, equivalently, of "understanding" [ἐπιστήμη μετὰ λόγος]) cannot be conferred on a single belief

[49]

taken in isolation (no matter how "real" its objects), but must instead be presented in appreciation of the place that belief occupies in a sufficiently wide and systematic body of other beliefs. In other words, Aristotle, like Plato, subscribes to the interrelational model. Hence, it would seem that so long as apprehensions of definitional ἀρχαί are considered as isolated bits and snatches of cognition, they will fall short of being knowledge in the unqualified sense.

If it is correct that Aristotle's rationale for denying that "merely universal" knowledge of ὅροι is the highest form possible is not just failure of existential import but also lack of systematicity, then it should be possible to see how, in the process of moving from this state to the actual production of syllogistic demonstrations, both failures are overcome. My central proposal is that the presyllogistic framing stage of demonstration is seen by Aristotle as accomplishing just that. It is a procedure wherein some set of Platonistic ὅροι that have been previously acquired (by the process described in *Posterior Analytics* 2.19) are then superimposed upon some scientifically interesting genus of individuals whose existence and place in the broader scheme of things has already been recognized or assumed. This procedure both organizes that genus into a branching explanatory structure and simultaneously generates a set of immediate predications, which are referential universals (and hence objects of de re knowledge) and can therefore serve as the ultimate premises in syllogistic demonstrations of nonimmediate connections within that genus.

Hence, when the immediate premises of a given science that emerge from the framing procedure are considered collectively, they can be seen to reflect a systematization of the basic truths about the subject-genus into an organized body of scientific knowledge in which explanations going all the way back to those fundamental premises can then be constructed. And this, as Burnyeat correctly argues, is the only form of cognition Aristotle thinks worthy of being called knowledge in the strictest possible sense, or as Burnyeat puts it, scientific understanding. Thus, it is possible to understand the remark at *Posterior Analytics* 1.2.71b18–20, that "knowledge in the unqualified sense comes from demonstration," as a distinctly Aristotelian specification of Plato's insight in the *Theaetetus* that genuine knowledge requires the possession of an interrelational logos. The difference, of course, is that whereas Plato simply identifies such logoi with the Platonistic definitions generated by division, for Aristotle these logoi are nothing less than the complete syllogistic demonstrations that (to reinvoke the language of *Posterior Analytics* 2.1 and 2) allow one to know not just *that* the fact in question is true, but also *why* it is true. For on the present interpretation, the construction of such an explanation (more specifically, the acquisition of its ultimate premises) requires that the demonstrator have already come to apprehend in a systematic manner all of the salient necessary interconnections obtaining within the field of study. In that sense, the demonstrative procedure as a whole can be said to reveal the systematic relations which the demonstrated item bears to other propositions (most importantly, the ultimate premises) within its appropriate science.

THE PRODUCTS OF DEMONSTRATION

According to Aristotle's own words at *Posterior Analytics* 1.2.71b9–19, knowledge "in the unqualified sense" (ἁπλῶς) is acquired "by means of demonstration" (δι' ἀποδείξεως). Now that the various sorts of ἀρχαί of Aristotelian demonstration have been explicated separately, we are finally in a position to see how they operate together to yield knowledge of the appropriate sort. That is, we can now say exactly what it is about the demonstrative process that makes Aristotle believe that its products should deserve the elevated status of knowledge ἁπλῶς. By way of contrast, let us recall one likely reason noted earlier for his insistence that possession of the substantive meaning assumptions of demonstration—what I have been calling immediate definitional assumptions—does not deserve this status. We saw above that the only sort of knowledge one can have of these starting points is (using the distinction of *Posterior Analytics* 1.1) "merely universal," and so is not "about" any individual existents that might happen to fall under its terms. By contrast, the immediate predications that emerge from the framing stage are not only universal in form but genuine referential universals (or hypotheses), and therefore can function as genuine demonstrative premises. It is these, and not the ὅροι from which they are generated, that Aristotle insists at 71b22 must be "better known" than the products of the entire demonstrative process. Moreover, it is these ultimate immediate syllogistic premises (rather than the "mere definitory reformulations" that Hintikka concocts[30]) that are the true source of the existential import that then percolates down to the ultimate demonstranda of Aristotelian science. In short, then, the conclusions of Aristotelian demonstrations are referential universal statements expressing mediated (that is to say, explainable) connections between terms.

But this, I have suggested, is only one of Aristotle's two independent reasons for according to demonstrative conclusions the title of knowledge *simpliciter*. The other stems from the thought, which I suggest is central to the epistemology of the *Posterior Analytics,* that such a conclusion is properly speaking inseparable from the demonstration supporting it. That is, Aristotle insists that epistemological value is determined, not by contemplating the proposition alone, but (to revive for a moment the old Platonic expression) by the proposition "together with its account" (μετά τοῦ λογοῦ). But since, according to its Aristotelian specification, the account in question is nothing other than the entire syllogistic demonstration of the proposition, and since, as we saw above, the premises of this demonstration are necessarily acquired by means of a divisional procedure that organizes the entire subject-genus into a taxonomic structure, it is a small and very natural step to conceive of knowledge of the demonstrated proposition itself as part and parcel of one's complete and systematic understanding of the whole genus in which it resides, and it is not hard to understand why Aristotle (like Plato before him) should want to make this sort of systematic understanding a necessary requirement for the possession of ἐπιστήμη in his own strictest sense of that term.

THE DEMONSTRABILITY OF DEFINITIONS

However, it may reasonably be wondered why, if the distinction between de re and "merely universal" knowledge is as central to Aristotle's theory of demonstration as I say, he seems to mention it only on the very outskirts of the *Posterior Analytics* (in Book 1, Chapter 1), where his concern is not yet to set out the theory but to motivate it by appeal to the broadest epistemological concerns. In other words, if I am right that the application of this distinction to definitional knowledge especially is crucial to understanding how genuine scientific understanding is fundamentally different from, and yet generated out of, preexistent knowledge of ἀρχαί, then presumably we should find him making explicit and highly visible applications of this distinction to mark off a difference between prescientific knowledge of pseudopredicational, definitional ἀρχαί not suitable for use in demonstration, and their derivative and genuinely predicational counterparts, which can serve as demonstrative premises.

Let me first say that this distinction is reflected to some extent throughout the *Posterior Analytics* by Aristotle's regular (if not religious) practice noted by Hintikka of reserving the term "definition" (ὅρος) to stand for what I am calling definitional ἀρχαί, and employing alternative terminology (usually "immediates" [ἄμεσοι] or "atomics" [ἄτομοι]) to refer to the immediate definitional predications that function as ultimate demonstrative premises. This in fact is the pattern of use evident in the two passages discussed above in *Posterior Analytics* 1.2 and 10, where he asserts that ὅροι (identified there as ἀρχαί) are not genuine *hypotheses,* but instead "mere *theses,*" on the ground that they make no assertions of existence or nonexistence.[31] In the view I am urging, this is tantamount to the assertion that such definitions cannot serve as demonstrative premises precisely because they do not carry existential import, and so, failing to "say one thing of another," [32] are not even authentic predications.

But it may still be objected that these passages at best provide weak circumstantial evidence that Aristotle sometimes *presupposes* the distinction I am ascribing to him. However, we will now be reminded that the original challenge demanded more: if the distinction in question is indeed pivotal to Aristotle's theory, then we should find him somewhere bothering to warn his readers of its presence and importance, and not simply writing as if it had already been made clear when in fact it had not.

Fortunately, it is not necessary to rely only on circumstantial evidence on this point, because there is a place where the distinction is set out in quite explicit terms. What is more, this occurs right where it would be most expected: in the much discussed (but still obscure) third through tenth chapters of the second book of the *Posterior Analytics,* where Aristotle addresses the question of precisely how definitions fit into the freshly exposited theory of ἀπόδειξις. The central concern of these chapters is precipitated by Aristotle's declarations in Chapters 1 and 2 that the production of demonstrative syllogisms can in some contexts suffice to answer a "What is it?" question. The issue then is to determine exactly how the "what-is-it" (τὸ τί ἐστι) of a given subject is "shown" (δείκνυται) by syllogistic demonstrations in the science that studies it (90a35–36). However, for reasons having to do with features of Aristotle's philosophical method, the initial stages of this investigation (Chapters 3 through 6) leave unexpressed and unquestioned the Platonic assumption of the *Sophist* and the *Statesman* that a definition is a statement of the τί ἐστι of its object, with the result that the discussion in its early stages moves back and forth indiscriminately between the original question of 90a35–36 and other distinct (though obviously related) questions about the place of definition in demonstration. Thus, for instance, after having argued in a preliminary way in Chapter 3 for the true (if unexciting) claims that the classes of definitions and demonstrable propositions are distinct, and that neither includes the other (91a8–12), Aristotle then turns in Chapter 4 to what he sees as the more interesting and difficult question of whether the two classes even intersect.[33] But as it is configured by the Platonic assumption mentioned above, the question actually posed at 91a13–14 is "whether there is syllogism and demonstration of the τι ἐστι."

It is not always appreciated how well, from this point on, Aristotle's procedure matches the general pattern of dialectical inquiry so beautifully exposited in G. E. L. Owen's landmark article, "Tithenai Ta Phainomena."[34] According to Owen's account, this sort of investigation characteristically opens with an "aporetic survey," in which a number of possible (and in many cases, actually propounded) answers to some loosely formulated question are subjected to close critical scrutiny. At some point after each of these ἐνδόξα has been shown in its turn to land in conceptual difficulty, Aristotle begins to set the stage for resolving these difficulties by recasting the original question into his own distinctive semitechnical vocabulary, in this way superimposing his own system of analytical concepts on the issues he is treating.

Now even the casual reader of Aristotle is aware that virtually every one of his key philosophical terms is equivocated upon as a matter of course, not just from treatise to treatise, but often within a single work, and sometimes even within a single chapter. This is not at all to charge him with sloppiness or indifference in his terminological habits. On the contrary, his patterns of equivocation are both systematic and deliberate, and moreover are highly valued by him as an indispensable part of the philosophical method he employs to bring about dialectical resolution of the conceptual problems uncovered in his aporetic surveys. For by translating a question under study into his own systematically equivocal language, he effectively disambiguates the question by separating out various of its possible interpretations, one of which in the usual case he identifies as the "strict" (κυρίως), "unqualified" (ἀπλῶς), or "primary" (πρῶτον) interpretation. Armed with this disambiguation, he is then in a position to produce what we might call the "full answer" to his question by giving what he takes to be the correct answer on each interpretation (with special emphasis, of course, on the primary interpretation). Finally, different parts of the "full answer" are deployed to show that each of the ἐνδόξα dealt with earlier went wrong because of a failure to respect subtle differences among the meanings of terms, but also that each is in fact a misfired attempt to express some portion of the whole truth contained in Aristotle's own final, enlightened position. Thus, in the end, all positions except Aristotle's are literally rejected, but all are nonetheless accomodated, and it is in this sense that he believes his method "saves the phenomena."

True to this general form, Aristotle's full answer to the question of whether there are any demonstrable definitions is that on some interpretations of the question there are, and on others not. Furthermore, it is not surprising that his specification of the various interpretations involved turns on exploiting ambiguities in the terms *definition* and *demonstration,* since these are conspicuously the only two available candidates for this role. To begin with, the "strict" or "primary" interpretation of the question and its associated answer are quite easy to spot. At 91a15ff. he argues in effect that while definitions are expressions of immediate connections between terms, the construction of a demonstration always proceeds by "finding the middle [term]" ($\zeta\eta\tau\eta\sigma\iota\varsigma\ \tau o\hat{v}\ \mu\epsilon\sigma o\hat{v}$) that links the two terms of the prospective conclusion (90a10). Hence, since, in the strict sense of the term, something can be said to be demonstrated only if it is the conclusion of a legitimate demonstrative syllogism, it follows straightforwardly that, since definitions express immediate connections, strictly speaking no definition can be demonstrated.[35]

The presence of this little argument in Chapter 4 is generally acknowledged among writers on the *Posterior Analytics,* but it is important to notice that it applies equally against the strict demonstrability of merely universal definitional $\dot{\alpha}\rho\chi\alpha\acute{\iota}$ and that of the immediate primary premises to which they give rise in the framing stage of demonstration. What is not so well known is that Aristotle gives an altogether different argument in *Posterior Analytics* 2.7, which goes on to distinguish between these two ways of expressing definitional connections by showing that only the latter are demonstrable in another, weaker, sense of that term. One intended purpose of Chapter 7 is to cancel, or rather to qualify, the Platonic assumption that had gone unchallenged in Chapters 3 and 4, namely that a definition always gives the $\tau\acute{\iota}\ \dot{\epsilon}\sigma\tau\iota$ of its subject. Now, however, it emerges that Aristotle's actual, more complicated view of the matter is that although there is a sense of $\ddot{o}\rho o\varsigma$ for which this is so, in another sense (indeed the primary one employed in *Posterior Analytics* 1.2 and 10) a definition is simply a "statement of what the name means" ($\lambda\acute{o}\gamma o\varsigma\ \tau o\hat{v}\ \tau\acute{\iota}$ $\sigma\eta\mu\alpha\acute{\iota}\nu\epsilon\iota\ \tau\grave{o}\ \ddot{o}\nu o\mu\alpha$).

The argument for separating these two senses, like so much of the *Posterior Analytics,* is conducted within the epistemological substructure of the theory of demonstration. Aristotle's concern at 92b4−34 is to reconcile two seemingly incompatible views he holds about the relative priority of definitional and existential knowledge. On the one hand, he insists repeatedly that (a) one cannot come to know *what* X is without knowing (either beforehand or concurrently) *that* X is, (in other words, that X exists; 89b33, 92b5, 93a4). But on the other hand, it is both a feature of his own theory of demonstration and an observation he makes independently about "actual scientific practice" that (b) a science must assume the meanings of its nonprimitive terms and prove the existence of their significata.

There is of course the general question, which will be deferred for the time being, of whether there is any way at all to incorporate these two ideas harmoniously into a single coherent theory, but Aristotle's concern at 92b4–34 is much narrower. His question there is whether (a) is consistent with a very special understanding of (b) according to which the assumptions of meaning it mentions are Platonic definitions (that is, logoi obtained by the method of διαίρεσις that give *both* the τι ἐστι and the τί σημαίνει τὸ ὄνομα) that also function as ultimate syllogistic premises.

Aristotle's answer to this question is negative, and although his reasoning in *Posterior Analytics* 2.7 is highly suppressed, it is possible to reconstruct in the light of his earlier assertion at *Posterior Analytics* 1.2.72a26–b5 that (c) the premises of a demonstrative syllogism must be "better known than" (γνωριμώτερον) and "prior to" (πρότερον) its conclusion. He now observes at 92b19–20 that according to "current manners" of defining (and here I believe he is referring to Platonic Division as well as the inductive manner of apprehending definitional connections described in *Posterior Analytics* 2.19), one who defines does not thereby prove the existence of the definiendum. Hence, if a product of such a method were allowed to occur as a better known premise in a syllogism that proved the existence of its objects, it would after all be possible to know (prior to the demonstration) the τι ἐστι of those objects without knowing that they existed. But this is precisely what is ruled out by (a).

How then does Aristotle himself propose to reconcile (a) and (b) in the face of (c)? As I have suggested, his crucial ploy is to insist on a separation of two senses of the term ὅρος: the primary one (employed in 1.2 and 10) in which it is merely a statement of what a name means, and a secondary (Platonic) sense in which it is also a statement of the what-is-it of whatever answers to the name. He is then able to claim that only the second sort of definition can function as a premise in demonstration, which in turn allows him to maintain (as part of his "full answer" in 2.10) that there is an attenuated sense of the verb "to demonstrate" (ἀποδείκνυμι) in which these definitions can be said to be demonstrated by virtue of their occurrence as demonstrative premises (2.10.94a1−19).[36] A negative corollary to the argument of *Posterior Analytics* 2.7, as I have reconstructed it, is that definitions in the strict or primary Aristotelian sense—that is, statements that simply give the τί σημαίνει of terms— have no business whatever in demonstrative contexts, and so cannot be demonstrated even in the attenuated sense just explicated. This too is part of the full answer Aristotle develops in *Posterior Analytics* 2.10. In fact, it is the part he anticipates in Chapters 2 and 10 of Book 1 when he characterizes ὅροι (here understood in the primary sense) as "mere theses" not capable of functioning as demonstrative premises.

However, Aristotle can have this position only if he can point to a process wherein knowledge of immediate premises is acquired subsequent to, or at the very least concurrently with, coming to know that the objects whose τί ἐστι they express actually exist. For this reason, it is a significant point in favor of the interpretation of Aristotelian demonstration offered here that it represents the framing stage in just this way: as a process in which immediate and definitional syllogistic premises are collected by the imposition of systems of previously apprehended definitional ἀρχαί upon genera of entities already known or supposed to exist.

DEMONSTRATION AND ANALYTICITY

There is an additional benefit to be gained from the present interpretation. An accurate understanding of the respective roles of de re knowledge of immediate premises, and merely universal knowledge of definitional starting points in the theory of demonstration makes it possible to clear Aristotle of the charge, which I shall call the *analyticity objection,* that he envisions a scientific program somehow capable of explaining empirical facts about the world wholly on the basis of first principles that are themselves analytic and thus devoid of factual content.[37] This objection is motivated by the fact that *Posterior Analytics* 2.19, the chapter in which Aristotle attempts to explain how the preexistent meaning assumptions of demonstration are acquired in the first place, seems to leave little doubt that he regards these definitional starting points as Platonistic according to the above distinction. This observation, which in itself is perfectly correct, is then supposed by Aristotle's critics to necessitate an unbridgeable schism within his theory of demonstrative science. In particular, it is thought that the analyticity of these principles makes them logically isolated both from the empirical facts they are supposed to explain and from the perceptual experiences that are said in *Posterior Analytics* 2.19 to generate them.

Let us address the second aspect of this charge first. The criticism here is that a Platonistic construal of the character of definitional ἀρχαί is somehow at odds with the empiricist account given at 100a15ff. of ἐπαγωγή, the process by which these starting points come to be known in the first place. Its obscure martial imagery aside, this passage does seem to say quite clearly that knowledge of definitional ἀρχαί is derived ultimately from multiple "perceptions" (αἰσθήσεις) of sensible particulars of the relevant kinds. But it is then to be wondered how the truth of analytic statements could possibly be apprehended by any such empirical process. More specifically, the worry is that because perception is in its essential nature a confrontation with a fully particular sensible object, no single perceptual experience could ever produce a cognitive state with universal content, nor could any merely combinatory operations upon any finite collection of such experiences.

The general argument that any necessary truth is analytic, and therefore known a priori, stems from an empiricist tradition (reaching back at least to Locke), which has tended to take an extremely narrow view of the nature of necessary truth. According to this view, if a sentence (a) does not express a contingent matter of fact about the actual individuals falling under its subject, then (no matter whether it is a logical tautology or a conceptual truth) it is (b) true solely by virtue of the meaning of its terms. As such, it is construed as (c) having no existential force with respect to individuals and as (d) making no factual assertions whatever, but merely as (e) expressing relations between ideas or meanings. But since, on this view, the truth of such a sentence is grounded, not in any objective features of the experienced world, but rather in the structural characteristics of some artifactual, conceptual, or linguistic system, it is reasoned that such a sentence (f) could not possibly be justified by appeal to perceptual experience.

Despite its long-standing popularity, this line of argument is a rather blatant non sequitur. For unless one begins with the extremely dubious assumption, presupposed by (e), that universal kinds are nothing but meanings residing in heads or lexicons, it simply does not follow that a sentence satisfying (a) will have *any* of characteristics (b) through (e). In particular, there seems to be nothing whatever improper in believing (as Aristotle in fact does) both that a sentence such as

(2) Every man is animal

can be construed as expressing a necessary relation between two natural kinds, and that these kinds along with their interrelations are objective features of the physical world, and not just reflections of our thought or language. But if this is plausible, there is no reason not to suppose what (f) denies: that one could (and indeed must) come to acquire knowledge of these necessary connections through perceptual acquaintance with the world in which they subsist.

Of course, this would pose a problem if one also subscribed to an ultra-empiricist theory of perception and knowledge according to which both the object and the content of a perceptual experience must be "perfectly particular." But this is precisely the kind of theory that Aristotle does not hold. It is true that he reacts vigorously to the Platonist's separation of universals from the visible world, but he is every bit as much a realist—albeit an immanent realist—as the target of those attacks. Consequently, his metaphysics allows him to analyze perception, as Plato cannot, as acquaintance not just with an individual substance, but also with the immanent universals which that substance instantiates, since they are for him actually present at the site of perception. In fact, he takes pains to remind his readers of this theory of perception parenthetically in the midst of his description of ἐπαγωγή in *Posterior Analytics* 2.19: "even though it is the particular (τὸ καθ᾽ ἕκαστον) which is perceived (αἰσθάνεται), the perception (ἡ αἴσθησις) is *of the universal* (τοῦ καθόλου), for example, [the perception is] of man, not of Callias, [who is] a man" (100a18–b2).

The use of the genitives at b1, in contrast to the use of the verb with direct object in the line before, is clearly intended as an intentional idiom. The point of the passage is that even though perception can rightly be regarded as a physical interaction with a concrete particular (the direct object of αἰσθάνεται), the immediate product of this interaction is a cognitive state with a representational function, the intentional content of which is universal in character. Thus, at least as far as his account of the acquisition of definitional ἀρχαί is concerned, there is no unbridgeable schism in Aristotle's theory between acquaintance with particulars and analytic knowledge of universals, for the simple reason that ground-level perceptual knowledge, on his analysis, involves acquaintance with (immanent) universals.

Of course, all of this is compatible with the other part of the analyticity objection, namely that there is in Aristotle's theory an unbridgeable schism in the opposite direction, going from knowledge of first principles of demonstration (however acquired) to the knowledge it is supposed ultimately to ground. The objection, in short, is that if the substantive, definitional starting points of demonstration are indeed analytic (that is, Platonistic) statements that can be known at best in the "merely universal" manner of *Posterior Analytics* 1.1, then they are logically incapable of entailing de re knowledge of particulars.

This objection, like the one considered above, rests on a failure to see that Aristotle's immanent realism cuts across the false dichotomies represented by descriptions (a)–(f) above. Again, on the ultra-empiricist attitude toward necessary truth, a true sentence is either about individuals (in which case it is contingent), or (taken exclusively) it is "merely analytic," in which case it does not reflect objective features of the world, and so must be known a priori. We already saw that the definitional ἀρχαί discussed in *Posterior Analytics* 2.19 constitute violations of this alleged division since they are not about individuals, yet they do represent objective features of the world (relations among kinds), and moreover do come to be known through perceptual experience. Now we can see in addition that the immediate premises of demonstration also violate the empiricist dichotomy, though for a different reason. Since they are referential universals, they *are* statements about the actual individuals which come under their subject terms, and so they obviously have factual content, and reflect objective features of the physical world. For as we saw above, they would be false if their subjects failed to refer, and would express different facts if their subjects referred to different individuals. Yet Aristotle would see none of this as reason to classify them as merely contingent. In fact, when a sentence like (2) is construed as a referential universal, it reflects essentially the same metaphysical circumstance, that is, the same necessary relation between immanent kinds, as does its Platonistic counterpart.

Once this last point is recognized, then it becomes clear exactly where the alleged unbridgeable schism between analytic first principles and the existentially "loaded" explananda of scientific demonstration is traversed in Aristotle's theory. My proposal is that the presyllogistic framing stage of demonstration is seen by him as a procedure for transforming merely universal knowledge of necessary connections among kinds into de re knowledge of these very same connections (and others as well). This is achieved by deploying a set of definitional ἀρχαί (previously acquired in the manner discussed in *Posterior Analytics* 2.19) upon a field of scientifically interesting objects (whose existence and place in the wider scheme have also been previously apprehended) so as to generate a set of existentially loaded premises expressing immediate and necessary connections within that field.

[60]

There is, then, a very important sense in which the question of whether the necessity operative in Aristotle's theory of demonstration should be construed as essentialistic or merely analytic is misconceived. The fact is that what he regards as the very highest form of knowledge possible is typically conveyed by a special sort of general sentence (the referential universal) that is about individuals and yet at the same time expresses necessary relations among the natural kinds to which those individuals belong. One way to put this is to say that such sentences express analytic (and a posteriori) truths about actual individuals, qua members of the natural kinds to which they belong. Hence, their necessity can be said to reside both in the analytic connections among those kinds and in the essentialistic connections between substantial[38] kinds and their actual members.[39] In epistemological terms, this means that knowledge of such necessary truths will require both previous apprehension of necessary relations among the kinds in question (that is, immediate definitional ἀρχαί), and the recognition (implicit in the framing procedure) that certain actual individuals fall under those kinds. To return full circle to the passage discussed at the very beginning of this chapter, this is exactly what is conveyed by the description of de re knowledge in *Posterior Analytics* 1.1 as "knowledge of what was known previously, and at the same time . . . of the things which happen to fall under the universal of which there is knowledge."

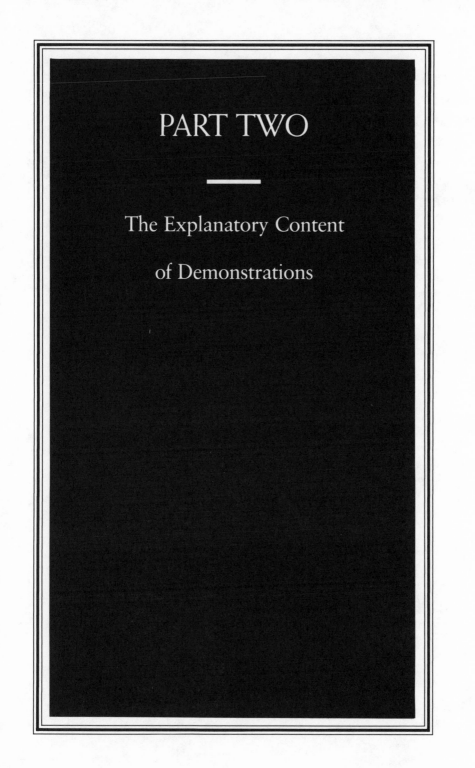

PART TWO

The Explanatory Content

of Demonstrations

THREE

———

The Character of Demonstrative

Premises

The account developed so far of the broad structure of an Aristotelian demonstration has dealt only with the logical character of legitimate demonstrative premises (in particular, with their existential force and extensional immediacy), but it has told us nothing about the sorts of terms Aristotle thinks can properly occur in such premises, and therefore nothing about the sorts of connections between terms that these premises are supposed to express. In short, we have not yet learned anything about the substantive content of demonstrations. This structural account by itself underdetermines Aristotle's theory because it leaves entirely out of account his insistence noted earlier that a demonstration must above all constitute an explanation. He clearly does not think that every syllogism composed exclusively of immediate premises is an explanation of its conclusion. For example, at *Posterior Analytics* 1.13.78a30–b4 he rejects the following syllogism as a legitimate demonstration:

    (i)   Every planet fails to twinkle, and
    (ii) everything that fails to twinkle is near, so
    (iii) every planet is near,

on the grounds that even if its premises are both immediate, it reverses the correct explanatory order between failure to twinkle and nearness exhibited in the genuine demonstration,

(i)   Every planet is near, and

(ii) every near thing fails to twinkle, so

(iii) every planet fails to twinkle,

and so cannot be said to reveal the "reason" (τό διότι) for its conclusion. Moreover, inasmuch as he regularly equates showing the reason for a proposition with finding, not just any middle between its terms, but one that constitutes a "cause" (αἴτιον; *Posterior Analytics* 1.2.71b9–16; 2.2.90a5–24), the problem Aristotle finds with the first syllogism, in the language of 71b20–26, is that although (we may assume) both of its premises are true, *immediate,* and therefore *primary,* it is nonetheless not a good demonstration because its minor premise, is not prior to, (objectively) better known than, or causative of its conclusion.

As I hope to show, Aristotle's strategy for ensuring satisfaction of these three remaining conditions, all of which pertain to the explanatory content of demonstrations, is reflected in his broad programmatic remarks in *Posterior Analytics* 1.10 when he indicates that a demonstrative science should confine itself exclusively to "per se" (καθ'αὑτό) attributes: "Proper (ἴδια) to each science are the subjects whose existence it assumes, and whose per se attributes (ὑπάρχοντα καθ'αὑτά) it studies. . . . Of these subjects both the existence (τὸ εἶναι) and the meaning (τοδὶ εἶναι) are assumed, but as for the per se attributes, only the meaning (τί σημαίνει) is assumed" (1.10.76b5–7). The central task of this and the following three chapters, then, will be to develop a detailed interpretation of Aristotle's doctrine of per se attributes, with the ultimate aim of showing how it provides the basis of his views about the explanatory force of demonstrations.

KNOWLEDGE AND NECESSITY IN THE *POSTERIOR ANALYTICS*

Throughout the *Organon* Aristotle gives numerous examples of sentences containing the modal-adverbial expressions ἀνάγκη and ἐξ ἀνάγκη. What is more, he has quite a bit to say in those works about the logical behavior of those expressions. For instance, in the twelfth and thirteenth chapters of *De Interpretatione,* he considers the interdefinability between "necessarily" and its correlative "possibly" (ἐνδεχόμενον); in the ninth chapter of the same work he points out differences in the scope of the "necessarily" operator between correct and incorrect versions of the Law of Excluded Middle; and in the eighth through the twelfth chapters of

Prior Analytics 1, he conducts a protracted and detailed investigation into the validity of various modal syllogistic inferences involving apodeictic, or "necessarily," sentences.

But for all this early interest in the subject of necessity, Aristotle never attempts to provide an explanatory, nonmodal analysis of apodeictic sentences until the *Posterior Analytics,* his treatise on the nature of "demonstration" (ἀπόδειξις), or scientific explanation. This coincidence of interest in science and necessity, according to Aristotle's own testimony, stems from his views about the objects of knowledge. Although his extant writings on general epistemology,[1] compared with those of Plato, are quite sparse, what there is commits its author without question to the Platonic doctrine enunciated in the *Theaetetus* that the only propositions (states of affairs or facts) that can be known (rather than merely believed) are those that "cannot be otherwise" (ἀδύνατον ἄλλως ἔχειν). This doctrine, which I shall refer to as the principle of *epistemic conservativism,*

> (EC) (For every p) if p is known to be the case, then p is
> necessarily the case,

is clearly evidenced, among other places, at *Posterior Analytics* 73a20 and 88b31, and *Nicomachean Ethics* 1139b20.

It must be admitted that Aristotle's reasons for holding (EC) are not very obvious. It is remotely possible that he comes to believe it by means of essentially the same modal fallacy Plato is sometimes accused of committing in the *Theaetetus,* namely that of confusing the highly controversial (EC) with another, more plausible (but less interesting) principle:

> Necessarily, (for every p) if p is known to be the case,
> then p is the case.

To be sure, *if* it were true, as some have suggested,[2] that Aristotle is inept concerning the correct placement of modal operators, then this mistaken inference might plausibly be attributed to him. However, it appears that these criticisms are not actually warranted by the evidence on which they are claimed to rest,[3] and it is in any case preferable to find an explanation according to which Aristotle's reasons for accepting (EC) are more systematic and deliberate. One especially plausible explanation of this sort has been offered by Hintikka,[4] who argues that Aristotle regards the truth of (EC) as required to ensure that all known truths are *eternal* truths, and that this latter doctrine is the natural outcome of the dual tendencies (in both Plato and Aristotle) to think of temporally indefinite sentences as paradigmatic vehicles of communication while at the same time analyzing knowledge as some sort of direct acquaintance between knowing subject and known object.

But however difficult it is to discover Aristotle's reasons for holding (EC), the effect of that commitment on the theory of scientific explanation set out in the *Posterior Analytics* is relatively easy to discern. At the beginning of Chapter 4 of Book 1, he prefaces an investigation into the nature of scientific premises as follows: "Since the object of scientific knowledge in the unqualified sense cannot be otherwise than it is, what is reached by demonstrative knowledge will be necessarily true. Now knowledge is demonstrative when we possess it in virtue of having a demonstration; therefore, the premises from which the demonstration comes are necessarily true" (73a21–25).

In light of some other early passages, the import of these remarks can be made out quite clearly. As represented by (EC), knowledge, most especially scientific knowledge, is of what cannot be otherwise, that is (according to *De Interpretatione* 13.22b5), of what is necessary. Now since, according to *Posterior Analytics* 1.2.71b17, demonstration is the justificatory procedure by which such knowledge is acquired, this means that the product of a demonstration must always be some necessary proposition. But since demonstration, according to *Posterior Analytics* 71b18, is a "type of syllogism," and its product (that is, its conclusion) is always necessary, it follows directly that its premises must be necessary as well (73a24).[5]

Right after elucidating this supposed implication of (EC), Aristotle declares at 73a25–27 that it is therefore desirable to comprehend the nature and character of the premises of demonstration, and he proceeds forthwith (in Chapters 4 through 10 of the first book of the *Posterior Analytics*) to look into that very matter, presumably with the aim of producing a general characterization of the necessary statements that can serve as premises in scientific syllogisms. Throughout the remainder of part 2, we shall be concerned to understand his views about the nature of these statements.

CATHOLIC PREDICATION

First of all, although this is not stated outright, it is clear enough that the background set from which Aristotle distinguishes the sorts of sentences he is interested in consists of true, indicative, present tense, declarative, affirmative, and simple subject-predicate sentences. For these are the only type of affirmative statements that can function in syllogisms, as can be seen through an examination of the various concrete examples and schemata given throughout the *Analytics*.[6] Within this background set, Aristotle then endeavors to define a certain subtype, which he calls "*catholic*" (καθόλου) *predications,* that can stand in scientific syllogisms. At 73b25–27, this feature is said to be a complex one involving three subconditions, each of which pertains to the nature of the relation between the subject and predicate parts of the sentence in question.[7] For the predicate of a sentence to be truly predicated καθόλου of its subject, Aristotle says, it must apply to that subject (i) "in every instance" (κατὰ παντός), (ii) "per se" (καθ'αὑτό), and (iii) "qua itself" (ᾗ αὐτό).

As I shall be interpreting them, subconditions (i) and (iii) both place essentially extensional requirements on catholic predication, and so are not centrally involved in questions about their necessity. They therefore may be dealt with briefly and put aside. When Aristotle says that the predicate of a given sentence must be truly predicated κατὰ παντός of its subject, he means that the attribute referred to by the predicate must apply to every single instance of which the subject is true. This should not be taken for a formal requirement that scientific premises must take the form of universal sentences, since many of Aristotle's own examples of scientific premises are singular sentences (see, for example, *Posterior Analytics* 2.11.94a37–b8), and any true singular sentence does meet the κατὰ παντός condition. Furthermore, another reason he needs to make this condition explicit is that his general theory of predication leaves open the possibility of what might be called indefinite sentences, for instance "Man is animal," that contain no article or restricting adjective to indicate whether they are to be taken as making an assertion about all, most, or merely some of what the subject term denotes. The proclivity to employ such sentences is very likely reinforced by the absence of an indefinite article in Greek. But even in modern English, where there is no such lack, parallel cases arise. For instance, while the sentence,

(1) Women drive racing cars

would in normal contexts be regarded as equivalent to an existentially quantified sentence, another sentence that seems quite similar to (1),

(2) Women possess two X sex chromosomes

apparently expresses a proposition about all women. Aristotle's subcondition (i), then, ensures that if an indefinitely quantified statement is to serve as a scientific premise, it must truly assert something about the entire extension of its subject term.

By subcondition (iii), which requires that the predicate of a καθόλου predication must be truly predicated of its subject "qua itself" (ᾗ αὐτό), Aristotle means to insist that not only must the predicate of such a statement apply truly (and per se, as will be explicated later) over the entire extension of the subject, but there must also be no class wider than the extension of the subject term (except possibly that of the predicate itself) to all of whose members that predicate also belongs (again, per se). In other words, it is not enough that the predicate of a true καθόλου sentence applies both κατὰ παντός and per se to its subject; it is also necessary that the subject of the sentence have the widest extension of any terms for which this is the case, with the possible exception of the predicate itself.

A good way to illustrate what this third subcondition of the condition comes to is the one chosen by Aristotle himself at 73b33−74a7. There he considers a sentence that meets both of the other subconditions but not the third. The example given is

> (3) Isosceles triangles have angles equal to two right
>   angles.

Now the property referred to by the predicate part of this sentence is plainly one that is had by all isosceles triangles, which ensures that the predication is κατὰ παντός. Further, let us assume that the predication is also per se (pending our investigation into that subcondition later). On the other hand, the sentence fails to be ᾗ αὐτό since there is a class of things (namely, *all* triangles) that includes the class of isosceles triangles, of whose entire membership the predicate of the sentence is also true. Hence, while the predicate of (3) is true of its subject both κατὰ παντός and καθ'αὑτό, it is not true of it ᾗ αὐτό, and hence the sentence is not καθόλου.

There is a certain ambiguity in Aristotle's discussion of the "qua itself" subcondition that deserves some comment. As interpreted above, it requires that there be no term wider than the subject, other than the predicate itself for which the predicate holds universally. By contrast, some writers have proposed a much stronger construal on which it requires that there can be no such term at all, including the predicate itself. On this interpretation the subcondition (and therefore the καθόλου condition as a whole) is taken to entail that all scientific predications must have coextensive terms, or in the terminology of the *Topics*, that they all must be "convertible" or "counterpredicable" statements.[8] The difference between these two interpretations does not show up very well in connection with sentence (3), since it fails to satisfy the subcondition on both. Consider, however, a sentence such as

(4) Every square is a rectangle,

which might be thought to express an immediate relation between its terms, but is not a convertible statement. On the weaker interpretation advocated here, (4) would be counted as satisfying subcondition (iii) (and in fact would count as καθόλου) since the only class that includes squares and to which the predicate applies is the class of rectangles itself (under this or some other description), while on the stronger interpretation the fact that every rectangle is a rectangle is enough to remove (4) from the field of legitimate scientific premises.

My preference for the weaker interpretation is based on what seems to me overwhelming evidence in the *Posterior Analytics* against the view that Aristotle conceives of demonstration as proceeding exclusively by means of convertible propositions (which incidentally has the curious consequence that the subject-matter of any Aristotelian demonstration would in effect be confined entirely to relations among coextensive predicates at a single divisional node). To begin with, it is significant that he never once says that his καθόλου condition entails convertibility or counterpredicability, even though he is quite comfortable using those terms not just in the *Topics* but also in the *Posterior Analytics* itself (for instance, at 90b35, 91a16, 36). In addition, this view of demonstration as concerned exclusively with coextensive terms would make it exceedingly difficult to understand the point of the very elegant arguments he gives in *Posterior Analytics* 1.19–23 to show that the possibility of finite demonstration is vouchsafed by the fact that any upward to downward sequence of immediate predicational links must contain only a finite number of terms. Indeed, he says quite clearly at 82a15 that such sequences would not even occur in cases where all terms are convertible. But by far the most telling objection to understanding the καθόλου condition as entailing convertibility is based on the observation that in a number of places Aristotle clearly allows demonstrations that contain nonconvertible premises. At *Posterior Analytics* 2.16.98b32, he says that if deciduousness belongs καθόλου to a certain whole (genus), then "if there are subspecies [of that genus, it can be shown that] deciduousness belongs καθόλου to them as well." For it is certainly impossible that a single attribute could be coextensive both with a certain genus and with one of its subspecies. In view of these difficulties with the alternative, it is preferable to interpret the "qua itself" subcondition in the weaker fashion so that it is satisfied not just by convertible predications (which are of course immediate, since there could be no middle between coextensive terms), but is in effect an alternative specification of the condition that scientific premises must be immediate in the general sense that there must be no term which intervenes *extensionally* between subject and predicate (that is, which is both wider than the subject and narrower than the predicate). Clearly, this condition is met both by convertible statements and by immediate and nonconvertible ones like (4).[9]

THE *PER SE* REQUIREMENT

On the basis of the account given in chapter 1 it should be clear by now how Aristotelian division (that is, the framing stage of demonstration) is sufficient to provide premises that meet both of the two extensional subconditions just discussed. To begin with, the fact that the method generates inclusion sequences of terms by itself entails that if A is an "ancestor" of B in the correct ordering, it will of necessity be true of all B. Moreover, Aristotle's procedure for ensuring that nothing is left out of the ordering of terms guarantees that, if B is next in order to A, there can be no terms that extensionally intervene between them, which is to say that A is also predicated of B qua itself. On the other hand, it was observed that Aristotle's discussion of this divisional method simply takes for granted that all connections between the terms involved are in some way or other nonaccidental, where that *intensional* requirement was left unanalyzed. I now want to suggest that in *Posterior Analytics* 1.4 this intensional condition on demonstrative premises is addressed by subcondition (ii) on catholic predications, namely that their predicates apply καθ'αὑτό to their subjects. Clearly, this is what is supposed to ensure the necessity of such predications, as Aristotle says quite plainly at 73b16−19: "Therefore, concerning things known in the unqualified sense, those things which are said to belong per se to their subjects, either in the sense that their subjects are contained in them, or in the sense that they are contained in their subjects, do so . . . of necessity." Then, after offering what appears to be an argument to support this, he reiterates the point at 73b24, by declaring that "thus, . . . per se attributes must belong to their subjects of necessity."[10]

In chapter 5 we shall try to understand exactly why Aristotle thinks that per se predications are necessary. Meanwhile, if we now put together what we have learned by examining various parts of *Posterior Analytics* 1.4, the results can be summarized as follows. Aristotle thinks that all sentences that can serve as scientific premises are necessary (73a21), and that their necessity is a consequence of their being per se predications. What we must do now is look carefully at the part of the chapter where Aristotle explicates the nature of per se predication so that we might gain from these remarks some insight into his reasons for thinking that such predications are necessary.

It will surprise no one familiar with Aristotle's philosophical prose that when we go to the passage where Aristotle first discusses what he means by the expression "per se" (*Posterior Analytics* 1.4.73a35–b16), we find that he actually presents not one but four separate explications of that term.[11] We may make the separation of these senses more graphic by performing some minor surgery on the passage: slightly reformulating some sentences into more precise language, physically separating the four different explications and their accompanying examples, excising superfluous examples, and attaching subscripted numerals to keep the four senses distinct hereafter. Here then is the postoperative version of the passage:

Type 1 (73a35–38):

X belongs per se$_1$ to Y if X is in the what-is-it of Y. Example: *Line* is in the what-is-it of *triangle,* so *line* belongs per se$_1$ to *triangle.*

Type 2 (73a38–b4):

X belongs per se$_2$ to Y if Y is in the what-is-it of X. Example: *Line* is in the what-is-it of *straight,* so *straight* belongs per se$_2$ to *line.*

Type 3 (73b4–10):

X is per se$_3$ if X is not said of some other subject. Example: [Primary] substance (or whatever else denotes some individual thing) is not said of anything other than itself, so [primary] substance is per se$_3$.

Type 4 (73b10–16):

X happens per se$_4$ to Y if X happens to Y in virtue of [Y] itself. Example: Death happens to a slaughtered thing in virtue of "the slaughtered" itself [that is, in virtue of a thing's being slaughtered], so death happens per se$_4$ to a slaughtered thing.

In the next three chapters, we shall look closely at these explications in order to identify the exact type of statement Aristotle has in mind in each case, with the ultimate aim of coming to understand Aristotle's underlying views about the explanatory function of demonstrative premises.

FOUR

———

Type 1 Per Se Predication

The substantive account of the nature of per se predication to be offered here is one according to which that doctrine is properly regarded as growing out of a seldom recognized rudimentary semantics for simple, subject-predicate, affirmative sentences, which I shall argue is implicitly contained in the first five chapters of the *Categories*.[1] My account therefore begins with an examination of those chapters.

THE SEMANTICS OF THE *CATEGORIES*

The doctrine from which the *Categories* takes its name is presented in Chapter 4 at 1b25 – 2a10:

> Of things said without any combination, each signifies either substance, or quantity, or qualification, or a relative, or where, or when, or being-in-a-position, or having, or doing, or being affected. To give a rough idea, examples of substance are man, horse; of quantity: four-foot, five-foot; of qualification: white, grammatical; of a relative: double, half, larger; of where: in the Lyceum, in the marketplace; of when: yesterday, last year; of being-in-a-position: is-lying, is-sitting; of having: has-shoes-on, has-armor-on; of doing: cutting, burning; of being affected: being-cut, being-burned.
>
> None of the above is said just by itself in any affirmation, but by

the combination of these with one another an affirmation is produced. For every affirmation, it seems, is either true or false, but of things said without any combination none is either true or false (e.g., "man," "white," "runs," "wins").[2]

The most immediate problem confronting a reader of this chapter is that of determining exactly what sort of things are classified by this division. Aristotle tells us explicitly that he is classifying "things said without combination" (τὰ κατὰ ἄνευ συμπλοκῆς λεγομένα), which Julius Moravcsik[3] has forcefully argued must be simple linguistic items, or terms. The argument is that when these items are combined, what result are sentences, and so the things that go into the combination must likewise be linguistic expressions. Moravcsik supports his claim that the products of combination are sentences (rather than some extralinguistic entities such as propositions) in two ways. First, he connects Aristotle's use of the term ἡ συμπλοκή to certain Platonic occurrences of the same term that quite clearly refer to an "interweaving" of words and phrases into sentences. Secondly, he argues that since Aristotle holds that the products of combination are "affirmations" (αἱ καταφάσεις), which are capable of being true or false, and since he also holds that it is only sentences that are capable of bearing truth-values, it follows that the materials of combination must also be linguistic entities.

These arguments are cogent enough, and they can be supplemented by the observation that the "things" classified in *Categories* 4 are entities that "signify" (σημαίνουσι) other things, which seems to be a function that could only be performed by linguistic items. But while Moravcsik is quite right that the distinction at 1b25–2a10 is linguistic, it should not be concluded that the items Aristotle groups under the various categories are themselves linguistic items. To think that is not to see the correct emphasis of the chapter, or of the *Categories* as a whole. For as John Ackrill says at the very beginning of his commentary on the work, "it is important to recognize from the start that the *Categories* is not primarily or explicitly about names, but about the things that names signify. . . . Aristotle relies greatly on linguistic facts and tests, but his aim is to discover truths about non-linguistic items."[4]

This point, which I shall argue later is slightly overstated, can be applied to the chapter in question as follows. The immediate objects of the classification announced at the beginning of Chapter 4 (and those which concern Moravcsik) are certainly linguistic entities. But it is just as important that this division of linguistic entities is wholly *semantical*. In classifying "things said without combination," which were identified above as terms, Aristotle makes no mention at all of their syntactical or grammatical properties. Rather, his sole way of distinguishing them is by reference to the different sorts of nonlinguistic entities they signify. In effect, then, the linguistic entities are classified vicariously under such headings as "things said without combination *that signify substances*," "things said without combination *that signify qualities*," and so forth. As such, the ostensive classification of linguistic items is but a thin veil for a more fundamental classification of their nonlinguistic significata, and this more fundamental division is the ontological doctrine of the categories.

One major reason this point is not always noticed, I think, stems from Aristotle's reliance on linguistic observations in constructing his list of categories. While the ontological division is logically prior to the linguistic classification of "things said without combination" (in the sense that each division in the former is wholly specified by reference to some division in the latter), Aristotle also seems to think, as Ackrill puts it, that "the identification and classification of these [nonlinguistic] things could . . . only be achieved by attention to what we say."[5] Thus it is easy to see how confusion about Aristotle's intentions can occur. For even though the immediate objects of the announced classification in the chapter are indeed expressions, and even though Aristotle's method of performing the classification centrally involves linguistic observations, the important work accomplished in the chapter is nonetheless metaphysical: the classification of nonlinguistic entities into ultimate ontological categories.

But let us now dig deeper into Aristotle's general purposes in writing *Categories* 4. We have just seen that his primary concern is to classify "things that are" (τὰ ὄντα) into their ultimate genera. But does this mean that his interests at that point are purely and simply in metaphysics for its own sake? Some doubt about this view arises from the concurrent interest in language in the same chapter, which has already been noted. If all Aristotle is doing there is classificatory metaphysics, then what is the point of his mentioning that there are simple expressions that signify items in each of the various categories, and that these simple expressions are capable of being interwoven together into sentences, which he says are the only things that can be true or false?

When Chapter 4 is taken by itself, these peculiarities do little more than raise the suspicion that Aristotle is not merely engaged in classificatory metaphysics as an end in itself. But when this chapter is put beside *Categories* 2, there emerges the positive view that the ontological doctrine of the categories in Chapter 4 is actually part of a larger effort to

provide what might be described as an informal semantics for simple affirmative subject-predicate sentences. In the first place, notice that Chapter 2 presents none of the difficulties of Chapter 4 in trying to decide
whether Aristotle is talking about words or things. It comes in two neatly
divided sections, the first of which is plainly about expressions, or "things
said" (τῶν λεγομένων; 1a16), and the second just as plainly about nonlinguistic entities, or "things that are" (τῶν ὄντων; 1a20). Moreover, if
we consider the sequence of the remarks made under these two headings,
the semantic interpretation just suggested is strongly indicated. First, at
1a15–20, Aristotle introduces and gives examples of the operation he
calls "combination" (ἡ συμπλοκή), which we saw above involves only
linguistic expressions. Then at 1a20–b20, he introduces and discusses
two relations—the *said-of* and the *inherence* relations—which are said
to hold between nonlinguistic items exclusively. Furthermore, from the
actual examples provided, we can also infer that some (and probably all)
of the things that can stand in these relations are the very things said in
Chapter 4 to be signified by expressions that undergo combination. If this
information is put together with what was extracted earlier from Chapter
4, it is then possible to identify a set of Aristotelian principles that may
quite plausibly be regarded as the rough outline of a semantical system:

> (S1) Simple, subject-predicate affirmative sentences
> (henceforth *atomic sentences*) are either true or
> false. (2a6–8)[6]
> (S2) Atomic sentences are constructed by combination
> out of exactly two uncombined expressions (hence-
> forth *sentential elements*). (1a15–20, 2a4–6)
> (S3) Each sentential element signifies some entity in one
> of the categories. (1b25–2a4)
> (S4) Some pairs of the entities signified by sentential ele-
> ments stand in the said-of relation, and others stand
> in the inherence relation.

All that is needed to make these principles into a fully explicit semantic for atomic sentences[7] is a statement that relates the truth of true
atomic sentences to the two ontological relations mentioned in (S4). Although there is no such truth analysis actually expressed in *Categories*
1–4, Montgomery Furth has plausibly reconstructed a partial one on the
basis of Aristotle's discussion of examples there.[8] According to this reconstruction, the analysis proceeds in two steps, which can be seen by considering any true atomic sentence, say one about Socrates. Such a sen-

tence will have the general form "Socrates is F" (or perhaps just "Socrates F," since in Greek the copula is dispensable), where F is some suitable simple predicate expression. The important thing to notice here is that substituends for F in this schema can include predicative (that is, verbal or adjectival) expressions such as "walks" and "(is) tall," as well as sortal nominal expressions such as "(is a) man." According to Furth, no matter what F signifies (and so, whether it is predicative or nominal), such a sentence can first be "thrown into a standard and canonical form, technical-ese: 'Fness is predicated of "κατηγορεῖται" of Socrates.'"[9] This canonical translation, on the Furth reconstruction, can then be further analyzed as expressing one or the other of two "deep structures": its truth will be explained, depending on what the original predicate F was, either by the fact that Fness is *said of* Socrates, or by the fact that Fness *inheres* in Socrates.[10]

It should be mentioned here that there are serious use-mention confusions involved in Aristotle's use of the verb "to predicate" (κατηγορεῖν) in *Categories*. He uses this term in such a wide-open sense that sentences containing it may or may not have subject terms that refer to linguistic expressions. For instance, at 2a8 he allows that *white* (which is said to be present in *body*, and is therefore nonlinguistic) is also predicated of *body*, whereas 2a20 clearly indicates the possibility that a "name" (ὄνομα) can also be predicated of a subject. In the absence of quotation devices, this dual use of the verb often produces great confusion in attempts to understand particular occurrences. For example, the sentence "*Animal* is predicated of *man*" at 2a38 could mean either that the genus animal is predicated of the species man, or that the term *animal* is predicated of man.

Fortunately, the verb *to predicate* occurs only in the intermediate stage of the semantical analysis we have been discussing, so its problems do not reach the critical aspect of that analysis, the disjunctive application of the said-of and inherence relations over the entire class of true atomic sentences. For Aristotle makes it clear that these are ontological relations that always stand between extralinguistic things signified by sentential elements, never between sentential elements themselves, and so his references to these relations are not infected by the ambiguity observed in his use of the verb *to predicate*. Therefore, the problems above with the verb κατηγορεῖν can be circumvented by simply collapsing the two steps into a single truth analysis from which the offending idiom has been eliminated:

> (S5) If "A is B" is true, then (where "A" signifies A, and
>   "B" signifies B) either B is said of A or B inheres
>   in A.

According to the semantical principles so far collected from *Categories* 2 and 4, each atomic sentence is combined out of two sentential elements, each of these signifies some item in one of the categories, and the truth value of the atomic sentence is determined according to whether the two significata stand (in the right order) in either the said-of or the inherence relation. But the semantical theory S_o is still not likely to be very informative until we have some more definite idea what these two relations are. Ackrill[11] has suggested that such information is not forthcoming in the *Categories* because Aristotle simply discovered the said-of versus inherence distinction in the ways of speaking current among his contemporaries. Now, if this were correct, we should regard discussions of the distinction as something like theoretically innocent reports of how language is actually used, and there would be no outstanding reason to scour the text in search of deeper explications of the relations that comprise it. There is, however, reason to be dubious about Ackrill's view. Evidence both in the *Categories* itself and in the writings of Aristotle's contemporaries[12] suggests that the expressions used to denote these two relations were in fact not commonly used as they are in *Categories* 2. For instance, Aristotle takes pains at 1a23 to caution his readers that when he says one thing is "in" another, he does not mean that the first is in the second *as a part*. This seems to be a warning that he is using a term that already has a familiar meaning in some different and technical sense.

But if the "said of" and "present in" terminology is indeed a piece of Aristotelian technical (or semitechnical) jargon, what is supposed to be the ultimate source of its intelligibility? The most obvious place to look for an answer is the so-called tetrachotomy passage (*Categories* 1a20–b9), in which the said-of and inherence relations are first introduced. In a slightly more natural order than that given by Aristotle, the tetrachotomy consists of four types of entity: (i) things that are neither said of anything, nor inhere in anything (1b3–9), (ii) things that are said of something, but do not inhere in anything (1a20–22), (iii) things that inhere in something, but are not said of anything (1a23–9), and finally, (iv) things that are both said of something and inhere in something (1a29–b3). An examination of Aristotle's examples in this passage together with his further comments in *Categories* 5[13] about the elements of the tetrachotomy at least reveals what he takes to be paradigm instances of each of these divisions. They are, respectively, the following:

(i) *Primary substances* (πρῶται οὐσίαι). These are individuals in the

Category of Substance, such things as "the particular man" (ὁ τὶς ἄνθρωπος) and "the particular horse" (ὁ τὶς ἵππος; 2a13–14).

(ii) *Secondary substances* (δεύτεραι οὐσίαι). These are what Aristotle
also sometimes refers to as genera (γένη) and species (εἴδη) in the Category of Substance, and are apparently said of both the individuals they
contain and the subordinate species they include.[14] The examples given
are "man" (ὁ ἄνθρωπος) and "animal" (τὸ ζῷον; 2a18).

(iii) *Nonsubstantial particulars*. These are the analogues of primary substances in the nonsubstantial categories, because they can only stand on
the right side of the said-of relation. They also inhere in primary substances. The examples given are "the particular [piece] of grammatical
knowledge" (ἡ τὶς γραμματική), which inheres in the (particular) soul,
and "the particular white" (τὸ τὶ λευκόν) which inheres in the (particular) body (1a27–28).

(iv) *Nonsubstantial universals*. These, finally, are the counterparts of secondary substances within the nonsubstantial categories. They are said-of
type (iii) entities, as well as their own subordinate types, and they inhere
in entities of both types (i) and (ii). Aristotle gives as an example of this
division "color" (τὸ χρῶμα), which he says inheres both "in body" (ἐν
σώματι) and "in a particular body" (ἐν τινὶ σώματι) and which presumably is also said of a particular color (2b1–6).[15]

However, even though it is easy enough to identify paradigm examples of each of these classifications, *Categories* 2 leaves quite a lot unsaid about the metaphysical nature of the four types of entities that make
up the tetrachotomy. In the case of type (i), primary substances, we can at
least get some clue by ostension, since the (presumably paradigmatic) examples given of this type, a particular man and a particular horse, are
quite easily recognized as concrete, individual, living things. Even in this
case, however, there is no more than a glimmering of the metaphysical
analysis to which Aristotle eventually subjects primary substance in the
Metaphysics.[16] And he tells us even less about the natures of the entities in
his three remaining divisions.[17] We may be pretty sure, given his repeated
railings against the Academy, that Aristotle does not regard universals
(that is, entities of types [ii] and [iv])[18] in a Platonic manner as separate
and self-sufficient existents, but there still remains a plurality of charac-
terizations of universals that are equally compatible with what little he
says about them in the early works.[19]

The most prudent course in the face of such paucity of information is
one of restraint. The fact is that Aristotle is not overly concerned in the

early works with metaphysics, and it is difficult if not impossible to import such concerns into them without relying on assumptions and concepts they do not actually discuss. For all we know, Aristotle simply did not confront the problem of determining the exact nature of universals (or for that matter, the exact nature of individuals) until later in his career. In accordance with these observations, I shall adopt a policy of evading these issues throughout this work, by simply underlining references to the entities of types (ii)–(iv) and leaving open the question about the natures of their referents.

However, even without knowing the exact nature of all of the types of entities divided by the tetrachotomy, we can discern in Aristotle's presentation of it the intended dependence of the said-of and inherence relations on his doctrine of the categories. Simply put, the said-of relation is such that its left term is always some higher kind in some category, and its right term is some kind or particular within the same category, whereas the inherence relation always has a primary or secondary substance as its right term, and some item in one of the nonsubstantial categories as its left term. These dependences can be distilled into the following two additional principles of the system S_0:

> (S6) If A is said of B, then A and B are homocategorial.
> (S7) If A inheres in B, then B is a substance, and A and B
> are heterocategorial (that is, A is a nonsubstance).[20]

To be sure, the distinction between necessary and contingent truth is not one of the explicit subjects of *Categories* 1–5, and I have not been meaning to claim otherwise. On the interpretation I have been defending, the sole function of the semantical theory (S_0) contained in those chapters is to specify the ontological conditions underlying the *truth* of all true atomic sentences. Even so, it would be hard to deny that some sensitivity on Aristotle's part to the distinction between necessity and contingency is reflected by the fact that S_0 does after all employ two different ontological relations (in contrast, for instance, to Plato's single participation relation) in order to accomplish this function.[21] For it is reasonably clear that the distinction between sentences whose truth is explained by the said-of and inherence relations coincides at least roughly with that between necessary and contingent truth. For instance, such "definitional" truths as "Man is animal," "Socrates is man," and "White is a color," will be analyzed in S_0 as expressing instances of the said-of relation, while merely accidental truths such as "Socrates is pale," will be explained in terms of the inherence of paleness in the subject. For this reason, it is not surprising that when Aristotle does have epistemological reasons in the *Posterior Analytics* to forge an explicit distinction between necessary and contingent truths, he turns to the bifurcated semantics of the *Categories* to provide the basis for that distinction. This, however, is not to say that he allows himself to carry the said-of versus inherence distinction as a whole piece into his theory of demonstration. On the contrary, it appears that matters become more complicated, and demands become greater, when the distinction between necessary and contingent truth moves into the center of his focus. We shall see presently that there are certain constraints operating in the *Analytics* that lead him to elaborate, and in some places even to modify, the simple two-part semantics of the *Categories*. During the remainder of part 2, I shall try to show how each of the four senses of *per se* just displayed can be construed as part of this procedure.

THE NEED FOR "INTRA-CATEGORIAL" DIVISIONS

We have seen that theory S_0 does provide an analysis of the truth of the atomic sentences of the *Categories*, but that it does so by making reference to two technical Aristotelian relations (the said-of and inherence relations) whose natures themselves stand in need of further explication. On the other hand, while the supplementary principles (S6) and (S7) do go some way toward explicating these relations in terms of the doctrine of the categories, they are both only one-way conditionals, and so at best supply some necessary conditions for the two relations. Hence, it follows that they together with (S5) do not fully explain the truth of either type of atomic sentence. For the categorial information contained in these principles does not by itself provide grounds for distinguishing genuine said-of predications such as

(1) Man is animal,
(2) Socrates is man,

from such false intracategorial predications as

(3) Man is Swaps,
(4) Socrates is a horse,

nor for distinguishing genuine inherence predications from contingently false statements such as

(5) Socrates is tall,

which satisfy the minimal categorial conditions specified by the right side of (S7). At its root, the problem here is that the categorial distinctions by themselves are simply too coarse to explain the truth of atomic sentences, and so must be augmented by finer intracategorial distinctions.

Aristotle never gives a general systematic treatment of the inherence relation, nor even attempts to do so.[22] This is probably because he saw a great many (if not all) instances of the inherence relation as the results of the operations of "chance" (ἡ τυχή). And in view of the disparaging things Aristotle says about the prospects of any scientific study of the fortuitous (for example, at *Posterior Analytics* 1.30.87b19–28), it is hardly surprising that he never attempted to give a completely general account of truths that he thought to be the results of its operation.

On the other hand, Aristotle does eventually say quite a bit more about the nature of said-of predications than what is given by (S6). In fact, I will now develop an interpretation of Aristotle's discussion of type 1 per se predication at 73a35–38 on which it identifies further conditions for the said-of relation. On the account I propose, these further conditions are not expressed in terms of the coarse ontological divisions of *Categories* 4, but rather in terms of finer, intracategorial distinctions that I shall argue are already implicit in the methodology Aristotle employs to develop his list of categories in the first place. As was mentioned earlier in connection with Ackrill, this methodology centrally involves Aristotle's exploitation of linguistic observations. It will now be useful to examine in more detail exactly how he uses such observations to arrive at his list of categories. Although there is not much indication in the *Categories* itself of how Aristotle does this, Ackrill[23] has found evidence in Chapter 9 of *Topics* 1 that he actually employs two distinct procedures that he apparently thinks yield identical results. Both can be thought of as linguistic in the sense that they involve considering the range of intuitively appropriate answers to certain questions, the main difference between them being that in one procedure different questions are asked about a single thing, while in the other a single question is asked about different things. Hence, I shall refer to the two procedures respectively as the *multiple-question* and the *single-question methods*. The nature of the two methods, and the differences between them, will come into view as I present each as an annotated set of directions for the construction of categories of being.

THE MULTIPLE-QUESTION METHOD

Step 1: Take before your mind a single primary substance, S (for example, a particular man or a particular horse).

It will be observed that this initial step presupposes the ability to distinguish between substances (more particularly, primary substances) and other types of entity. Apparently Aristotle is thinking of the categories as constructed by this method in his discussion of the tetrachotomy in *Categories* 2, since in that discussion also he seems to take the substance versus nonsubstance distinction as an unquestionable and unanalyzable fact.

> Step 2: List the most basic (most general) questions that
> can be asked about S.

The actual list of such basic questions Aristotle thinks will be produced in this step are: "What is it?" (τὶ ἐστί;), "How is it?" (ποῖος;), "How much is it?" (πόσος;), "What relation does it stand in?" (πρὸς τί;), "Where is it?" (ποῦ;), "When is it?" (πότε;), "In what attitude is it?" (τὶ κεῖται;), "In what state is it?" (τὶ ἔχει;), "What is it doing?" (τὶ ποιεῖ;), and "What is being done to it?" (τὶ πάσχει;). There is a minor problem at this point with Ackrill's description of the method. It seems that if steps 1 and 2 are to yield a complete list of such basic questions, then the initial choice of the substance to ask about will be crucial to the method. For if the initial choice of S were, say, a boulder, then presumably the ninth question would not appear because rocks do not *do* anything. Or if S were one of the numbers (which Aristotle sometimes thinks of as substances), then the fifth question (Where is it?) would not appear.

There are two different ways to get around this difficulty without drastically altering Ackrill's reconstruction. We might simply regard the method as an idealization in which steps 1 and 2 are performed for every substance, thus insuring a complete list. Alternatively, it may be that the initial choice of S really is crucial to the method, and that what is to be chosen is not just any substance, but a paradigmatic substance. This second alternative is at least hinted at by the fact that the substance Aristotle himself seems to choose is a particular man, the sort of thing which he generally regards as the most important and interesting kind of primary substance.[24]

> Step 3: Corresponding to each of these most basic questions, construct an ontological classification (that is, a category) consisting of entities signified by the predicate parts of the appropriate answers to that question.

Here I have made reference to the "predicate parts" of the answers simply as a concession to the peculiar feature of written English that questions are usually answered by complete sentences. By contrast, there is no rigid requirement in written Greek (or for that matter, in colloquial English) that meaningful responses have both a subject and a predicate, and so it is very likely that Aristotle thinks the questions on his list can be answered, fill-in-the-blank style, by responses of one or two words. For example, the question, "What is it like?" can be answered sufficiently by the single word "white." This means that Aristotle could very naturally think that things falling into the category generated by a certain question are those things signified by *whole* answers to that question.

What is required for an answer to be appropriate to a question in this method will again depend on whether the method is taken as an idealization or not. If it is, and the first two steps are understood to be performed on every substance, then only correct answers need to be counted as appropriate ones. On the other hand, if the method is not an idealization, and steps 1 and 2 are to be performed only on a single (paradigmatic) substance, then in order to achieve an exhaustive classification of "all existents" (πάντα τὰ ὄντα), it would be necessary to regard all possible correct and incorrect answers as appropriate.

THE SINGLE-QUESTION METHOD

Step 1: Take before your mind all the things there are.

This of course is going to be an idealized method. Practically speaking, if Aristotle employed this method at all, he probably attempted to gather just a suitably representative sample of entities. Also, it must be kept in mind that "all the things there are" (πάντα τὰ ὄντα) must be taken here in the most inclusive sense possible to include not just objects but also such things as qualities, locations, states, actions, and so forth.

> Step 2: Select one of these and ask "What is it?" (τὶ
> ἐστί;).[25] Give the most informative correct an-
> swer to this question, if there is one. Your an-
> swer, if there is one, should take the form "It is
> ———."[26] Now consider the thing signified by
> the predicate part of this answer and ask of *it*,
> "What is it?" and answer this question. Your an-
> swer should again take the form "It is ———."
> Repeat this step until you have finally asked a
> question which has no answer.

Let us call such a completed sequence of questions and answers a *chain,* and represent it by a vertical list of the signifying terms that occur in it, ordered so that the last term to occur is topmost, and let us refer to the chain which is initiated by asking about some entity X as X's Chain.

It might occur to the reader here that in some cases this step cannot be completed (that is, that some chains might be infinite). This apparent possibility also occurs to Aristotle (in a slightly different context), and he constructs a proof in *Posterior Analytics* 1.19–22.(81b29–84b20) to eliminate it.[27] Further, the possibility of performing this step in a way that produces consistent results presupposes that for each entity there is exactly one appropriate answer (or, as Aristotle puts it at *Categories* 5.2b7–13, one "most informative" [γνωριμώτατον] answer) to the question "What is it?" While this might seem to us quite dubious, Aristotle apparently endorses some doctrine of natural kinds which he believes will insure this result.

> Step 3: When step 2 has been performed for each member of the original collection, construct an ontological classification (a category) A for every expression "A" which occurs topmost in one or more chains.

Thus, for instance, if you find (as Aristotle apparently does) that the chain initiated by asking "What is it?" of a particular color ends with the same question being asked (but not answered) about quality in general, you then construct a category of Quality.

> Step 4: Finally, put into each category A all of the items signified in all of the chains in which "A" occurs topmost.

Some examples should show how this method is intended to operate. Suppose that among your original collection there are the following items: (i) Socrates, (ii) a particular horse (say, Swaps), (iii) the species man, (iv) a particular color (say, white$_{212}$), (v) a particular taste (say, sourness$_{109}$), and (vi) the general color white.[28]

Let us then imagine that the chains generated by performing step 2 on these items are represented as follows:[29]

(i) *Socrates' Chain*
    (a) substance
    (b) body
    (c) living body
    (d) animal

(ii) *Swaps' Chain*
    (a) substance
    (b) body
    (c) living body
    (d) animal

(e) footed animal
(f) two-footed animal
(g) man
(iii) *Man's Chain*
  (a) substance
  (b) body
  (c) living body
  (d) animal
  (e) footed animal
  (f) two-footed animal
(v) *White's Chain*
  (a) quality
  (b) sensible quality
  (c) visual quality
  (d) color

(e) footed animal
(f) four-footed animal
(g) horse
(iv) *White$_{212}$'s Chain*
  (a) quality
  (b) sensible quality
  (c) visual quality
  (d) color
  (e) white
(vi) *Sourness$_{109}$'s Chain*
  (a) quality
  (b) sensible quality
  (c) taste quality
  (d) sourness

Now since the topmost expressions in chains (i)–(iii) are "substance," and the topmost expressions in chains (iv)–(vi) are "quality," in order to perform step 4 you put all of the items signified by expressions in (i)–(iii) in the category of Substance, and all those signified by expressions in chains (iv)–(vi) into the category of Quality.

It will be observed that there are some items, such as footed animal, which get put into the same category more than once, as it were. This is because certain segments of different chains are identical. In fact, more can be said: if a single item ever appears in any two chains, the Aristotelian assumption that there is always a unique answer to the "what is it?" question entails that the two chains in question will be identical from the shared item up. This is the fact on which the medievals traded when they constructed what came to be known as the "tree of Porphyry" out of this Aristotelian doctrine. Although there is no evidence that Aristotle himself actually conflated chains in this manner, it is easy enough to see how he could have. If we simply regard any two like-membered chain segments as a single segment, we will in effect construct a hierarchical, or inverted tree structure out of Aristotle's classification. Moreover, the requirement of step 3 that all chains whose contents are included in a given category possess a common topmost member, plus the Aristotelian uniqueness assumption just mentioned, and the additional assumption that each uncombined signifying expression signifies exactly one entity, together insure that the Aristotelian categories are arranged into mutually independent strict hierarchies.[30]

As mentioned above, each of the two methods of generating categories requires supplementary assumptions in order to guarantee identical results across separate implementations. Furthermore, there are grounds for doubting that the two methods must, or even can, yield the same classifications.[31] I shall not worry over these difficulties here, since my main concern is not with the intrinsic merits of these methods or with the plausibility of the doctrine of the categories. The preceding remarks have been offered simply as a preparatory stage to seeing how deeply implicated the doctrine of the categories is in Aristotle's refinement of the *Categories* semantics in *Posterior Analytics* 1.4.

POSTERIOR ANALYTICS 73a35–38: TYPE 1 PER SE PREDICATION

The key piece of terminology in the explication of type 1 per se predication at 73a35–38 is the peculiar little noun-phrase, "the what-is-it" (τὸ τί ἐστιν). Ackrill has put forward the quite plausible view that Aristotle has a vacillating attitude toward his categories, at some times thinking of them as generated by one of the two methods, and at other times as by the other. Further, according to Ackrill, these vacillations are responsible for an otherwise puzzling inconsistency in Aristotle's use of the expression "what-is-it" in *Topics* 1.9. At 103b23 he apparently treats this expression as if it were simply synonymous with "substance" (οὐσία), since he uses it as a name for his first category (for which he usually reserves the name "Substance"). Yet just a few lines later in the same chapter, he uses the same expression in a way that is apparently much wider: "One who indicates the what-is-it of a thing, sometimes indicates a substance, sometimes a quality, and sometimes something in the other categories" (103b27–29).

Ackrill accounts for this terminological instability by hypothesizing that in the two locations Aristotle is influenced respectively by the two different methods he employs to construct his categories. In the narrower use of the term at 103b23, his choice of language is influenced by his thinking in terms of the multiple-question method, where the only appropriate answers to the "what-is-it?" question are ones that signify substances, since that question is only asked about (primary) substances in that method. Hence, in this frame of mind he could quite naturally think of the phrase "what-is-it" as a synonym for "substance." On the other hand, the wider use of the expression at 103b28 "clearly indicates," in Ackrill's words,[32] the single-question method, in which the "what-is-it?"

[89]

question is asked about every sort of entity, and so can properly evoke answers that signify items in any of the categories.[33]

Against this background, I want now to suggest that if the explication of type 1 per se predication at *Posterior Analytics* 73a35–38 is recognized as a place where the expression "what-is-it" is used in the wider sense of *Topics* 1.9, and hence as an allusion to the single-question method, then Aristotle can be seen in that passage to have elaborated upon the rudimentary semantical system S_0 of the *Categories* by supplying the finer, intracategorial, distinctions necessary to give sufficient conditions for the said-of relation.

Let us first get a more precise understanding of this wider use of the what-is-it. Ackrill himself does not say anything on this subject beyond the remark quoted above. However, by exploiting the above description of that method, it will be possible to provide a clearer explication. In the occurrence at *Topics* 103b28, as well as its many occurrences in *Posterior Analytics* 73a35–b16, the expression "what-is-it" is part of definite noun phrase formed by putting a neuter singular article in front of it. The whole phrase is then a nominalization of the "what-is-it?" question that plays the title role in the single-question method. Now on the basis of what we know about that method, we can make a pretty fair guess what meaning Aristotle intends the noun-phrase to have. When he refers to the what-is-it of some item Y, he is using a very natural shorthand for referring to the entire class of entities signified during the course of completing the entire sequence of questions and answers initiated in step 3 of the single-question method by asking "What is it?" about Y. In other words, in this shorthand, X is in the what-is-it of Y just in case X is signified by one of the expressions that occur in Y's chain.

We also saw earlier that the items contained in each Aristotelian category are ordered in a strict hierarchy, and now we know the identity of the relation that so orders them. It is the relation (which I shall refer to as relation E) expressed by sentences of the form: X is in the what-is-it of Y. If, now, the occurrence of "what-is-it" in our postoperative version of the explication of type 1 per se predication at *Posterior Analytics* 73a35–38 is taken as an instance of this wider use, the first glimpse of Aristotle's refinements on the theory S_0 emerges.

In our initial discussion of S_0 we saw that homocategoriality of subject and predicate by itself does not distinguish false homocategorial sentences from genuine said-of predications, and that finer, intracategorial distinctions were therefore needed. Now we can see that in the *Posterior Analytics* Aristotle has such finer distinctions in hand in the form of the hierarchical structure of the contents of the categories as ordered by relation E. Some homocategorial pairs, such as ⟨man, Socrates⟩ stand in this relation, while others, such as ⟨Swaps, man⟩ do not. Further, relation E, unlike mere homocategoriality, is sufficient for the truth of sentences that express it. This is because step 2 of the single-question method calls for only *correct* answers to the "what-is-it?" question. Thus, every predication in which the predicate occurs in the chain of the significatum of the subject is true. And since, as we just saw, X is in the what-is-it of Y just in case X is signified by an expression in Y's chain, it then follows that if X stands in relation E to Y, then any atomic sentence whose subject signifies Y and whose predicate signifies X will be true. Hence, Aristotle has all the semantic equipment necessary to analyze the truth of sentences such as "Socrates is man" without at the same time committing himself to the truth of false sentences such as "Socrates is horse." For while *man* is clearly in the what-is-it of Socrates, *horse* just as clearly is not.

My suggestion, then, is that the first type of per se predication explicated at *Posterior Analytics* 1.4.73a35−38 is a close descendant of the said-of relation in the *Categories*,[34] and that Aristotle supplies in that passage what is missing from the *Categories,* a statement of sufficient conditions for the said-of relation in terms of intracategorial ontological divisions. Moreover, it is these finer-grained divisions he has in mind when he insists in *Prior Analytics* 1.27−32 and *Posterior Analytics* 2.13 that the organization of a subject-genus, prior to syllogistic demonstration, by what I have called Aristotelian division must systematize the attributes in the what-is-it of their respective subjects.

Now since it has already been remarked that Aristotle sees no hope of giving a general systematic account of the only other type of true atomic sentence recognized in the *Categories* (those expressing the inherence relation), it might seem that there is now no room for futher improvements on S_0. This, however, is not the case. For while Aristotle is apparently quite content in the *Categories* to divide all true atomic sentences exhaustively into the two types dealt with by (S5), in *Posterior Analytics* 1.4 he evidently finds this classification (like the categorial distinctions themselves) too restrictive for his purposes. In particular, he there recognizes the existence of other types of true atomic sentences that do not, for various reasons, fall neatly into the twofold division of the *Categories.* In fact, I shall go on to argue that his explication of the remaining types of per se predication in that chapter can be understood as his attempt to modify his theory of predication to make room for these misfits.

FIVE

———

Type 2 Per Se Predication

PARTICIPATION IN THE *CATEGORIES*

Besides giving an informal semantics for atomic sentences in *Categories* 1–5, Aristotle there also offers some observations about the distinctive logical behavior of said-of predications by formulating two conditions that he takes to be characteristic of this sort and not shared by inherence predications. One of these is fairly straightforward. Chapter 3 opens with a statement of the transitivity of the said-of relation: "Whenever one thing is predicated of another as of a subject, all things said of what is predicated will be said of the subject also" (1b9–10).[1]

Now inasmuch as transitivity is a purely formal property that does not distinguish the said-of relation from a whole host of others, it will not play a central role here. However another, more substantial, condition is given in Chapter 5 at 2a19ff: "If something is said of a subject, both its name and its logos are necessarily predicated of the subject. . . . But as for things which are in a subject, in most cases[2] neither the name nor the logos is predicated of the subject."

Following Aristotle's own way of referring to this condition at *Topics* 121a11–12, we may call this condition *participation*.[3] In order to see exactly what it amounts to, we must first note that both conditions are evidently meant to apply to the *colloquial* atomic sentences whose truth is explicated by theory S_0 (that is, such combined expressions as "Man wins," and "Man [is] animal") and not to what Aristotle regards as the more perspicuous *canonical* expressions that inhabit instantiations of the right side of (S5):

> (S5) If "A is B" is true, then (where "A" signifies A, and
> "B" signifies B) either B is said of A or B inheres
> in A.

In light of this, the participation condition can be seen to be essentially grammatical. For while the canonical counterparts to said-of and inherence predications alike are formed by joining pairs of nominal expressions by means of the technical locutions of "is said of" (καθ'ὑποκειμένου λέγεται) and "inheres in" (ἐν ὑποκειμένῳ ἐστιν), there is a significant lack of parallel between the surface grammar of the two types of colloquial sentence. The predicate part of a colloquial said-of predication, such as

> (1) Man is (an) animal,

or

> (2) Socrates is (a) man,

is typically a nominal form (or, as we might specify further, a *sortal* expression, though this classification is not so obvious in a language lacking the indefinite article). Colloquial inherence predications, on the other hand, have as their predicate parts adjectival or verbal forms.

But why does Aristotle elect to express this grammatical distinction by means of the participation condition given at 2a19? The answer to this, I believe, lies in the fact that in the *Organon* only nominal forms (roughly, ὀνόματα) are what may be legitimately replaced by defining logoi. This is apparently a consequence of Aristotle's tendency to think of the objects of definition as things rather than expressions.[4] In the case of a typical said-of predication, the predicate is already in nominal form, and therefore the applicability of the defining logos to what is signified by the subject follows unproblematically from Aristotle's oft-repeated insistence that an adequate definitory logos is always substitutable for the name of what it defines.[5]

But now consider the case of a typical inherence predication,

> (3) Socrates (is) generous.

Here things are not so simple. If substitutivity of definitional equivalents were allowable for adjectival expressions as well as ὀνόματα, then this sentence would satisfy the participation condition, since the phrase that would be the definitional equivalent of "(is) generous" (perhaps, "tends to give freely of himself") is true of Socrates if (3) is true. But this is not Aristotelian. For him the fact that the phrase "(is) generous" is adjectival means that it is not a name and therefore has no definitionally equivalent logos. What can be defined, on the other hand, is the entity signified by "(is) generous," namely the ἕξις *generosity;* and its defining logos (say, "the propensity to give freely of oneself") is itself a nominal form, and as such is intersubstitutable with the name "generosity." Thus, Aristotle's point in saying at 2a28 that in the case of a predication such as (3), "neither the name nor the *logos* is predicated of the subject" is that both

> (4) Socrates is generosity,

and

> (5) Socrates is the propensity to give freely of oneself,

are false or worse.[6]

DIFFERENTIAE IN THE *CATEGORIES*

It appears that when Aristotle comes to forge a distinction between necessary and contingent truth in *Posterior Analytics* 1.4 (with an eye toward isolating those nonaccidental predications suitable for use in demonstrations), one reason he finds theory S_0 less than adequate to his purposes is that he now recognizes a type of sentence that does not fall neatly into the crude said-of versus inherence dichotomy. These are true sentences containing sentential elements which signify differentiae (διαφόραι), such as

> (6) Man (is) two-footed.

To be more precise, there are actually two distinct, though closely related, difficulties occasioned by the evident meaningfulness of such sentences. One is the semantical problem of providing an adequate explanation of their truth conditions. The other, whose eventual solution will have a direct bearing on the first, is the ontological problem of saying where differentiae fit into the classificatory metaphysical scheme of the *Categories*.

Even before considering his reactions to them, it is not hard to guess how Aristotle could have found himself in the midst of these difficulties. In the *Topics* and elsewhere, his favorite manner of definition is *per genus et differentia*. Moreover, inasmuch as this style of defining is the heart of the method of division practiced by Plato in the *Sophist* and *Statesman*, it must surely be counted as part of the baggage Aristotle carried away from the Academy. But it often happens that there is a price attached to Aristotle's acceptance of Platonic doctrines. In this case, he thereby commits himself to recognizing the truth of sentences like (6) and therefore to the existence of such "things" as "two-footedness." Thus, in order not to sacrifice the generality of the *Categories* program, he is forced to find a place for both of these in that framework. What we have here in effect is an instance where what Aristotle takes over from Plato comes into conflict with his own independently developed doctrines. Moreover, I shall argue presently that despite Aristotle's confident statements to the contrary, this conflict is not really resolved in the *Categories*.[7]

It is true that in *Categories* 5 (3a21–28) we do find the pronouncement that differentiae are said of the species they differentiate, and this, by (S6), would entail that differentiae are homocategorial with those species. Furthermore, there is no mystery about why Aristotle should want this to be so. Since reference to a differentia is as much a part of the definition as the name of the genus (according to the Platonic legacy), then surely differentia predications should be accorded a treatment that respects their status as definitional (and necessary) truths and does not dump them unceremoniously into the class of accidental inherence predications.

But for all this, there are also very powerful reasons why Aristotle is not free simply to classify differentia predications as said-of predications. Chief among these is the fact that they do not really satisfy the participation condition. Aristotle does quite a bit of pushing and pulling trying to get such sentences to pass this test, but in the end (as Ackrill points out[8]) these efforts must be regarded as so much desperate cosmetics. Briefly, his trick is to test for satisfaction of this condition only after first putting the differentia predication through the regimentation phase of the truth analysis discussed in chapter 4, so that (6) is recast as

(6') Two-footedness is predicated of *man*.

Following this regimentation, a differentia predication comes out containing only nominal forms, and in this form such predications certainly do satisfy the participation condition. However, this maneuver is only open to Aristotle at the cost of having to dispense with the participation condition altogether. For there is nothing to prevent exactly the same move in the case of a paradigmatic inherence predication. For instance, one could use virtually the same reasoning just displayed to show that sample sentence (3) satisfies the participation condition by first throwing it into the regimented form

(3') Generosity is predicated of Socrates,

and then arguing that the logos of generosity is substitutable for its name in (3′) without loss of truth. At base, the difficulty is this: since differentia predications are like inherence predications (and unlike said-of predications) in the respect that their predicates are typically not sortals, then Aristotle's heroic efforts notwithstanding, the fact is that differentia predications will satisfy the participation condition only if inherence predications satisfy it also. Hence, insofar as Aristotle is unwilling to give up the participation condition as a means of distinguishing the two types of sentence treated by theory S_0, he cannot legitimately treat differentia predications as expressing the said-of relation.

POSTERIOR ANALYTICS 73a38–b4: TYPE 2 PER SE PREDICATION

The principal contention of this chapter is that Aristotle was somewhat more successful in treating differentiae in the *Posterior Analytics,* and that his explication of type 2 per se predication at 73a38–b4 can plausibly be interpreted as a place where this better treatment occurs. Admittedly, this passage does not contain anything more about the relation between differentia and differentiated species—indeed, discussion of that matter is put off until the *Metaphysics*[9]—but it does at least go some way toward specifying the relation between a differentia and the genus whose species it differentiates.

Aristotle specifies the latter relation by invoking an observation he makes in the *Topics* about differentiae that has been largely misunderstood. At *Topics* 4.6.128a26, Aristotle states that differentiae (or more accurately, terms that pick out differentiae) always signify a "qualification of a genus" (ποιότητα τοῦ γένους). This point is then illustrated by the observation that a person who uses the expression "footed," which signifies a differentia, thereby signifies "some qualification" (ποιόν τι) of the genus *animal.*

Because of the occurrence of the expression ποιόν (as well as its proper nominal form ποιότητα) here, and the fact that this is the same expression used in the *Categories* to designate the category of Quality, this passage has understandably led some to the mistaken view that Aristotle puts all differentiae into that category,[10] which would unhappily suggest that they must inhere in their respective differentiated species. But despite this somewhat unfortunate choice of terminology, Aristotle's point here in fact has nothing at all to do with his theory of categories.[11] Rather, it is simply an observation of the pretheoretical fact about language that expressions signifying differentiae are always definable by expressions of the form, "a qualification of Φ," where Φ stands for the name of the genus whose subspecies the differentia in question differentiates.

It appears that in the explication of type 2 per se predication, Aristotle incorporates this observation into his conception of necessary definitional truth by expanding the notion of a what-is-it for differentiae. This expansion comes naturally if one thinks of the what-is-it of X quite generally as the set of things referred to in giving an exhaustive answer to the question, "What is X?" For while, on this understanding, the what-is-it of an individual or a kind will contain everything of which it is a member or a subkind (that is, everything signified in the chain generated for it in the single-question method exposited in the last chapter), the what-is-it of a differentia, on the other hand, will contain nothing more than the genus which it divides. To use Aristotle's example, if one were to ask "What is footedness?" the complete answer, "a qualification upon the genus animal," would make reference to just a single entity, the genus animal. Of course, one could ask the further, obviously relevant, question, "What is animal?" but in so doing one would, strictly speaking, have moved away from the original question about footedness and taken up instead the new question: "What is that of which footedness is a qualification?" Now since the what-is-it of a differentia is always single-membered in this way, its logos will always contain just one name: that of the genus of which it is a qualification.[12]

It will be recalled that the problem detected in the *Categories* was that differentia-predications did not fall cleanly on either side of the said-of versus inherence distinction presupposed by (S5). Aristotle there wanted to regard them as definitional and necessary truths, but they failed to satisfy an essential condition of the only definitional truths countenanced by his theory of predication S_0. We can now see that in *Posterior Analytics* 1.4 he gets around this difficulty by repudiating the simple dichotomy of the *Categories* and making room for another definitional relation besides the said-of (type 1 per se) relation, one that holds between a differentia and the genus it divides.[13] That he is able to describe these two relations in a way that makes them appear to be the inverses of one another, and so to give the doctrine of per se predication the appearance of having more unity than it actually possesses, can be credited to a combination of luck and ingenuity.

It might well be interjected at this point that the solution just outlined to the problems of differentiae is really no solution at all. For while I have argued that Aristotle was at least able to say something about the relation between differentia and divided genus, he seems to have left untouched both the original semantical problem of explaining the truth of species-differentia predications such as

(6) Man is two-footed,

and the original ontological problem of fitting differentiae such as *two-footedness* into his categorial scheme of things.

This complaint is well founded. I do not think that Aristotle's ultimate solutions to these problems are contained in the works I have been discussing. Instead, those solutions, which constitute the doctrine of the unity of definition, come with his recognition that the ontological problem of differentiae is not a genuine problem at all, because differentiae do not need a place in the hierarchical framework of the categories. This is because differentia terms do not signify a distinct class of ὄντα that must themselves be divided into genera and species. They simply denote the ways in which genera are divisible into species (which is to say, in the language of *Topics* 128a26, that they denote "qualifications upon genera"). As such, differentia are not themselves subject to categorial classification; they are simply the principles by which such classification is accomplished.

Along with this dissolution of the ontological problem comes a way of dealing with such species-differentia predications as (6). For since differentiae are now regarded as the principles by which specific division proceeds, there is obviously a one-to-one correspondence between species and differentiating differentiae. This point is recognized explicitly by Aristotle at *Metaphysics* 7.12.1038a17. From there it is but a small step to saying that each differentia term somehow specifies (not to say signifies) the species it differentiates, and in fact Aristotle apparently equates species and differentiae in much this way at *Metaphysics* 1038a19. On this understanding, sentence (6) could be thought of as logically equivalent to "Man (is) man," and so as necessarily true.

In any case, we are not so much interested here in Aristotle's final solution to the problems of differentiae as with discerning how his attempts to deal with them influences his characterization of definitional truth in the *Posterior Analytics*. The explication of types 1 and 2 per se predication at 73a35–b4, since they are expressed in the material mode, can be represented as containing refinements on the semantic treatment of definitional truth implicit in the *Categories*. For we may now replace truth definition (S5) with one that recognizes *three* distinct types of ontological configuration that might underlie a true predication:

(S5′) If "A is B" is true, then (where "A" signifies A, and "B" signifies B) either

(i) B is in the what-is-it of A (that is, B belongs per se₁ to A), or

(ii) A is in the what-is-it of B (that is B belongs per se₂ to A), or

(iii) B inheres in A (that is, B belongs both per accidens₁ and per accidens₂ to A).

THE NECESSITY OF PER SE PREDICATIONS

It was noted in chapter 3 that Aristotle locates the ultimate source of the necessity of scientific premises in their per se character. But since four separate senses of *per se* are explicated in *Posterior Analytics* 1.4, we need to know which of these Aristotle is employing when he says that per se predications are necessary. Does he, in other words, intend his point to apply to just some of the various distinct types of per se predications he discusses at 73a35–b16, or is it supposed to apply right across the board? The answer to this question is to be found in the explanatory statement that immediately follows Aristotle's final restatement of the per se requirement at 74b6–7. Right after declaring that per se predications are necessary, at b7–9 he gives as the reason for this (employing the explanatory particle γάρ) that in such predications either the predicate belongs in the what-is-it-of the subject, or vice versa. Now it is far from obvious how this by itself is supposed to explain why such per se predications should be necessary, but a simple comparison of this remark with 73a35–b4 leaves little doubt that Aristotle is here making an unambiguous reference to only the first two types of per se predication.[14]

It should be kept in mind here that because there are two distinct types of sentence involved, there is no reason to believe at the outset that the same sort of necessity attaches to both. Indeed, there is evidence indicating just the opposite conclusion. At *Posterior Analytics* 73b16–19, Aristotle offers an expanded version of the thesis of 74b6–9: "for it is not possible that they [type 1 and type 2 per se attributes] should *not* belong [to their subjects] either *absolutely* or [in the manner of] *the opposites*. For instance, either *straight* or *curved* belong to *line;* either *odd* or *even* to *number*" (*Posterior Analytics* 73b19–22, emphasis mine).

Besides the familiar logical point that necessity is definable in terms of possibility and negation (*De Interpretatione* 22b5), the information conveyed by this earlier passage is surely that every type 1 or type 2 per se attribute belongs to its subject with one of two kinds of necessity: such predications are said to be necessary "either absolutely or [in the manner of] opposites" (ἢ ἁπλῶς ἢ τὰ ἀντικείμενα).[15] Moreover, it appears that Aristotle does not intend the distinction between these two types of necessity to cut across that between the two kinds of predications. All four of the attributes he uses for illustration in the last sentence of the passage are generally regarded by him as examples of "opposites" (ἀντικείμενα), in fact, *odd* and *even* are explicitly mentioned as such at *Categories* 12a7, while at the same time each of them is also among the examples of type 2 per se attributes given at *Posterior Analytics* 73a40. This by itself shows that the class of type 2 per se attributes at least intersects the class of opposites and is perhaps included in it. Put beside the additional fact that none of Aristotle's examples of type 1 per se attributes is ever referred to by him as an opposite, this gives us enough reason to surmise that the two distinctions in question are perfectly juxtaposed—that Aristotle thinks of type 1 per se attributes as "absolutely" necessary, and type 2 per se attributes as necessary "in the manner of opposites."[16]

But what exactly are these two kinds of necessity? To my knowledge, there is no passage in the *Analytics,* or for that matter anywhere in the *Organon,* where he elaborates to the least degree on his bareboned remark at 74b22 that type 1 per se predications are "absolutely necessary."[17] Perhaps this is because he thinks this type of necessity is so familiar that it should be readily understood without explanation, or perhaps his references to it are meant to reflect some manner of speaking current among his contemporaries. A more likely hypothesis, however, is that even if he realizes in these early writings that much more can (and must) be said on this topic, he simply has not yet reached the point of formulating the pertinent questions, let alone working out his answers to them.[18] It was suggested in chapter 2 that in the *Posterior Analytics* he sees the necessity that attaches to definitional truths as grounded both in analytic relations among general (natural) kinds, and in essentialistic connections between primary substances and their proximate species, but that he does not clearly recognize at that point that there are two different relations involved. This stands in marked contrast to Books Z–Θ of the *Metaphysics,* which distinguish between the genus-species and kind-member relations, and focus on the latter (conceived there as the relation between a "composite" individual and its "substantial form," or "essence"). Hence, there is reason to suspect that this issue is so intertwined with the general problem of giving a satisfactory account of Aristotle's essentialism that its resolution must await a sorting out of the complex tangle of philosophical doctrines that comprise the central books of the *Metaphysics*.

But whatever the reason for the virtual lack of edification from Aristotle on the nature of the absolute necessity of type 1 per se predications, the prospect of apprehending the reasons behind his insistence that type 2 per se attributes belong to their subjects necessarily "in the manner of opposites" is initially much more promising. In the lines that follow immediately upon the articulation of the general thesis at 73b19–22, he offers the following explanation, which is clearly supposed to apply only to type 2 per se attributes: "For [the opposite of a given attribute] is the contrary, or the privation, or the contradictory [of the attribute] within the same genus. For instance, not-oddness is evenness within [the genus] number, inasmuch as the first entails the second. So, since it is necessary that everything be affirmed or denied, [type 2] per se attributes are necessary" (73b22–24).

Even though this explanation is mystifying in some respects, at least its initial assumptions are fairly evident. To begin with, if the εἰ at b24 is plausibly read as "since" instead of "if," then it is fairly clear that Aristotle's conclusion depends ultimately on what seems to be some modalized version of the *Law of Excluded Middle* (LEM) embedded in that clause, "since it is necessary that everything be affirmed or denied" (b24).

Now it was seen in chapter 1 that this law is one of the background assumptions required both by Platonic Division and by the adaptation of that method which Aristotle incorporates into his own theory of demonstration. Indeed, it is plausible to understand the main subject of *Posterior Analytics* 73b22–24 as a special sort of necessity that he takes to be uncovered by such divisional procedures. However, it will emerge in chapter 7 that both Plato and Aristotle have serious doubts about the meaningfulness of the law in an unrestricted form where it applies to every subject and every attribute whatsoever.[19] Consequently, Aristotle for his part tends always to understand and apply the principle only in restricted form. In fact, his application of the law at 73b22–24 appears to be doubly restricted. In the first place, it conforms to his general position, announced at *Posterior Analytics* 1.11, 77a22–26, that the law is meaningful only when restricted to subjects within some specified genus, in this case the genus *number*. But more than that, in this particular context it is also applied to a very special sort of attribute, which Aristotle refers to as "opposites," among which we have already seen he includes type 2 per se attributes. Whenever he presents examples of opposites, they are invariably given in pairs (which I shall call "A-pairs") such as (*odd, even*), (*straight, curved*), and (*healthy, diseased*), each of which exhaustively divides up the members of some genus. Let us say that a given A-pair is *appropriate to* the genus it so divides. Furthermore, the language of this passage indicates that Aristotle is interested here in pairs of attributes that carve out natural and necessary partitions within their respective genera.[20] For this reason it appears that he is relying not on the relatively weak modal form of the LEM:

> WEAK MLEM: Necessarily, for every member x of G, and
> for every attribute F applicable within G,
> x either has F or lacks F,

which would hold generally for any attribute that could be meaningfully applied within G, but rather on the considerably stronger thesis:

> STRONG MLEM: For every member x of G, and for every
> opposite F appropriate to G, x either
> necessarily has F or x necessarily lacks
> F.[21]

The evidence for this is to be found in another feature of opposites that Aristotle invokes at 73b23: "E.g. Not-oddness is evenness within [the genus] number, inasmuch as the second is entailed by (ἕπεται) the first." This suggests that he sees the division effected by A-pairs as sufficiently nonaccidental to support the very strong intensional relations of *property-identity* and *property-entailment*. That is, the possession of one opposite in an A-pair by a member of the appropriate genus is said here to be entailed by, and even tantamount to, that individual's lacking its partner. Hence, the modal character of the divisions effected by opposites is apparently seen by Aristotle as sufficient to underwrite his use at 73b23 of a restricted substitutional premise which I will refer to as the *Principle of Opposites:*

> (PO) If (Φ, Ψ) form an A-pair appropriate to genus G,
> then applications of "Ψ" and "not Φ" *within* G
> are intersubstitutable.

In employing this principle he evidently means to distinguish this type of dichotomy from the accidental sort that might be sustained temporarily, if say, all men were for a time either sitting or standing to the exclusion of all other physical attitudes. For, as Aristotle is no doubt aware, this latter transient state of affairs would not justify conflating the properties of *sitting* and *not-standing* within the human species, nor would it even justify the assertion that these properties entailed one another.

Aristotle's argument, then, is that STRONG MLEM and (PO) together with the implicit assumption that any pair of type 2 per se attributes form an A-pair of opposites, yield the conclusion that such attributes belong necessarily to the members of the genus to which that A-pair is appropriate. As it applies to the pair *odd* and *even,* Aristotle's actual example at 73b22–24, it purports to show that because these two attributes form an A-pair appropriate to the genus *number,* it follows that they belong necessarily to numbers.

But which numbers in particular? It is not yet clear what exactly the argument is supposed to show. In the passages quoted above (73b16–19, 24, 74b6–7), Aristotle's conclusion is represented as the thesis that a certain group of attributes belong necessarily to their subjects. However, in view of the fact that the announced primary purpose of *Posterior Analytics* 1.4 is to isolate a class of necessary *statements* that can function as syllogistic premises in demonstration (73a21–5), we still must ascertain precisely which statements comprise the sort of predication argued to be necessary at 73b22–24. Virtually all of the examples of type 2 per se predication in *Posterior Analytics* 1.4 are given in the form of indefinite or unquantified sentences such as:

(7) Odd belongs to number.
(8) Even belongs to number. (73a39–40).

Such sentences may be right at home in *Categories* (compare 1b38ff.) where Aristotle is interested only in specifying the ontological configurations that underlie various sorts of true predication. But the centerpiece of the *Analytics* is the syllogistic and its use in scientific demonstration, so we know that Aristotle's real concern at 73b22–24 is to demonstrate the necessity of a certain sort of syllogistic premise. These will have to take one or the other of the two general affirmative forms, "All Φs are Ψ," and "Some Φs are Ψ," which are actually dealt with by the logical theory of the *Prior Analytics.*

What remains, then, is to determine exactly which sentences Aristotle has in mind when he uses sentences like (7) and (8) to exemplify type 2 per se predication. To begin with, the simplest and most obvious way of disambiguating (7) and (8) can be rejected straightaway. If these sentences were understood as simple universal affirmatives,

(7a) All numbers are odd,

(8a) All numbers are even,

then we would have Aristotle arguing for the necessity of sentences that are plainly false, and necessarily false as well. Upon noting this, Jonathan Barnes suggests in his notes to *Posterior Analytics* 73a38–b4 that the import of Aristotle's conclusion that *odd* and *even* belong to numbers "necessarily *in the manner of opposites*" (73b19–22) is nothing more than the obvious truth that *one or the other* of this pair of attributes necessarily belongs to each and every number.[22] In other words, Barnes views the argument as designed to establish the necessity of a class of universal affirmative sentences that make *disjunctive predications*, in this case,

(9) All numbers are odd or even.

This view claims some initial credibility from the fact that the necessity of sentences like (9) is in fact entailed straightforwardly by the premises of the argument. On this reconstruction, the argument presumably commences with a valid application of WEAK MLEM [23] to the attribute *odd* and the genus *number*,

(10) Necessarily, all numbers are odd or not odd,

to which (PO) is then applied to yield the necessity of (9). Barnes's view also accords well with *Categories* 12a7, where Aristotle expressly affirms the necessity of (9). But despite its prima facie plausibility, there are two independently conclusive reasons why Barnes's interpretation of the argument cannot stand.

The first of these is that sentences like (9), involving as they do disjunctive predication, simply do not have the requisite form to serve as syllogistic (and hence demonstrative) premises. This difficulty apparently worries Barnes himself, judging from what he says in his notes to 73a35–b4 directly after proposing to read (7) and (8) as equivalent to (9): "Nevertheless, such disjunctive examples are not easily read into 73a37–40 . . . : they do not seem to 'say one thing of another' (cf. 72a9); and they are likely to be, at best, rare in the sciences" (115). But even this modest claim with which Barnes closes his discussion is not in fact supported by the texts. The use of sentences like (9) in Aristotelian scientific reasoning is not just rare; such sentences never occur as premises in demonstrative syllogisms. Not one of Barnes's purported examples of this allegedly rare occurrence proves on close reading to inhabit a genuine syllogistic context.[24] And this total lack of textual support for Barnes's view cannot be explained away by hypothesizing some eccentric narrowness in Aristotle's choice of examples. There are a number of passages in the *Analytics* (for example, *Prior Analytics* 24a16, and *Posterior Analytics* 72a9) that explicitly prohibit the use of anything but simple two-term (that is, single-predicate) sentences as syllogistic premises. Barnes's view therefore requires us to understand *Posterior Analytics* 1.4 as containing a rather blatant case of *ignoratio elenchi*, because it has Aristotle at 73b22–24 endeavoring to support his thesis that certain demonstrative premises are necessary (73a21–25) by arguing for the necessity of a group of sentences that do not and cannot function as premises in demonstration. Any proposal that assigns such a blunder to Aristotle should be regarded as an absolutely last resort.

There is another equally compelling reason that Barnes's interpretation of the argument cannot be right. It represents Aristotle as believing that his conclusion, that all numbers are necessarily odd *or* even, is somehow expressible by his statement (73b19, 24, 74b7) to the effect that *each* of these attributes, *taken separately,* is necessarily possessed by numbers. This would involve Aristotle in some variant of the modal fallacy of supposing that the necessity of a disjunction somehow distributes to its disjuncts. Yet he explicitly identifies and rejects this fallacious form of inference in his discussion of the future sea battle at *De Interpretatione* 9.19a29–33: "I say, for example, a sea battle must either take place tomorrow or not. No necessity is there, however, that it should come to pass or that it should not. What is necessary is that either it should happen tomorrow or not." Barnes is evidently aware of these difficulties, for he seems in the end to regard his proposal as no better than the best in a bad lot. Consider his final words on the subject: "Retaining the simple predicate 'odd,' we might try taking not number, but a kind of number as subject—e.g.: 'Every product of [two] odds is odd.' But there is no smell of this in the text" (115).

Let us pause now and identify the adequacy conditions for the task at hand: an altogether satisfactory interpretation of *Posterior Analytics* 1.4 should specify a class of Aristotelian sentences that both (a) involve the simple and separate predication of type 2 per se attributes such as *odd* and *even* so that they are well formed for syllogistic purposes, and (b) are shown to be necessary by the premises of the argument at 73b22–24. Barnes evidently believes that there are no sentences that satisfy both of these conditions, and then reasons that his account should prevail by default inasmuch as it at least respects condition (b) by representing 73b22–24 as containing a valid (if misdirected) argument for the necessity of sentences like (9). I shall now endeavor to obviate this maneuver by showing that there are in fact Aristotelian statements that satisfy both (a) and (b).

When Barnes rejects the proposal that condition (a) might be saved by understanding the type 2 per se predications in question to be sentences about certain kinds of numbers, he presumably does so on the grounds that the relevant text contains no subject-terms that could reasonably be thought to signify such narrower subkinds. Thus, when he says in particular that there is "no smell in the text" to indicate that Aristotle is thinking of such sentences as

(11) Every product of odds is odd,

it is no doubt because the only general terms that occur in Aristotle's discussions at 73a38–b4 and b22–24 are "odd," "even," and "number," and Barnes sees no way to construct a sentence out of these alone which is not about numbers generally, but only some kind of number.

It is significant that Barnes here leaves entirely out of account the most natural and straightforward way of understanding sentences (7) and (8) as syllogistic predications. For there are a number of passages in the *Prior Analytics* where Aristotle makes it clear that indefinite predications should as a matter of course be treated as particular statements (compare 26a30, 32, 39, b3, 29a28).[25] According to this convention, (7) and (8) would be equivalent to:

(7b) Some numbers are odd.
(8b) Some numbers are even.

Although Barnes doesn't consider these sentences explicitly, I suspect he rejects them out of hand as legitimate examples of type 2 per se predication on the grounds that while they are no doubt true (and even necessary), their necessity does not seem to follow from the premises of the argument at 73b22–24, which would mean that they fail condition (b) above. This I believe is yet another result of the misguided tendency to understand Aristotelian general sentence forms as translatable into modern quantifier logic.[26] On such an understanding, sentence (7b) for example, is an existentially quantified statement, so that its necessity would consist in the fact that the intersection of odd things and numbers is necessarily inhabited. Admittedly, it is very hard to see how this could follow from any form of MLEM (which is a universal statement about the logical structure of the field of numbers, and says nothing about whether any parts of that field are filled) together with some substitution rule. But this has little to do with Aristotle, for his particular statements are not existentially quantified.

Recall that I argued in chapter 2 that even though "Every S is P" entails "Some S is P" in Aristotle's logic, one cannot represent this by simply paraphrasing an existentially "loaded" Aristotelian universal statement as a conjunction of its universally quantified counterpart with an existentially quantified statement asserting the nonemptiness of its subject term. Rather, it was suggested, such a sentence should be understood as expressing a multitude of singular propositions, and so, as carrying corresponding presuppositions of singular existence for each of the individuals involved in those propositions. The key element in that analysis was that Aristotelian universal premises are to be treated, like singular statements, as having discrete subject terms with referential functions. Now a parallel point can be made for the Aristotelian particular statement. On this general way of understanding the relation between existence and predication, just as "every S" is a term that purports to refer to every one of the actual Ss, so "some S" should be regarded likewise as a discrete referring term whose purported reference is some subset of all the actual Ss.[27] Hence, it is plausible to surmise that in addition to the sort of sentence that was described as the "referential universal" in chapter 2, Aristotle's logic also recognizes a category of statement that we might call the *referential particular*.[28]

However, if (7b) and (8b) are now understood as referential particulars, it then becomes very easy to understand how Aristotle could see them as the statements whose necessity is at issue at *Posterior Analytics* 73b22–24. For STRONG MLEM and (PO) together imply:

> (12) Every number is necessarily odd or necessarily even.

Construed as a referential universal, this sentence asserts *of each and every number* either that it is necessarily odd or that it is necessarily even, which means that the singular propositions it expresses are divided into two types. That is to say, one half of the singular facts that make this whole sentence true are comprised by the (necessary) possession of oddness by certain subset of numbers (namely, the odd ones), while the other half involves the (necessary) possession of evenness by the remaining numbers. But these two distinct sets of singular propositions can also be expressed respectively by

> (13) Some numbers are necessarily odd,

and

> (14) Some numbers are necessarily even,

where these are understood as instances of the referential particular. Hence, since on these construals (13) and (14) are implied by (12), it is possible to understand *Posterior Analytics* 73b22–24 as concerned with the necessity of (7b) and (8b).[29]

SIX

———

Type 3 Per Accidens and Type 4

Per Se Predication

POSTERIOR ANALYTICS 73b6–8:
TYPE 3 PER ACCIDENS PREDICATION

For each of the two senses of per se Aristotle explicates at *Posterior Analytics* 1.4.73a35–b4, he also introduces and defines derivatively a complementary sense of "per accidens" (κατὰ συμβεβηκός). That is, something is said to be per accidens in a given sense, just in case it is not per se in the corresponding sense. I shall now argue that Aristotle's discussion of the third sense of these two expressions at 73b6–8 differs from those of the other three in that the recalcitrant sentences he is concerned to fit into his theory in that passage are not, as in the surrounding passages, a certain type of per se predication, but rather a certain type of per accidens predication. I shall first identify the troublesome "accidental" predications involved, and then show how 73b6–8 can be viewed as an attempt to deal with them.

An examination of S_0, and especially of (S7),

> (S7) If A inheres in B, then B is a substance, and A and B
> are heterocategorial (that is, A is a nonsubstance),

reveals that the theory sets very definite limits on the possibilities of intercategorial predication. The only such sentences countenanced are those in which a nonsubstantial entity is predicated of a primary or secondary substance. In particular, there is no possibility within that theory of a true intercategorial predication whose subject signifies a nonsubstance. However, there is conclusive evidence in the *Posterior Analytics* (and in the *Metaphysics*) that Aristotle recognizes the existence of such sentences, and that he thinks them to be in some sense (to be explained below) per accidens. For example, at *Posterior Analytics* 1.19.81b24 he says that the sentence

(1) The white (τὸ λευκόν) is (a) man[1]

is a per accidens predication, while the sentence

(2) The man is white

is not. Much the same point is expressed at *Metaphysics* Γ.4.1007b3 where Aristotle pronounces the following two sentences per accidens:

(3) The white is cultured.
(4) The cultured is white.

Notice that sentences like (1), (3), and (4) pose no great difficulties for modern philosophical theories of language because such theories invariably make use of two distinct types of semantical relations. One of these types, which I shall call *context-independent,* consists of those that hold simply between *expression-types* and extralinguistic entities.[2] Familiar examples of this sort of relation are the naming, denoting, and meaning relations. The other type, which I shall call *context-dependent,* consists of those that hold between expression-tokens and extralinguistic entities. Context-dependent relations, of which the most familiar is the reference relation, can be described either straightforwardly as two-place relations between tokens and the extralinguistic relata, or in a more complex manner by specifying an expression-type, the extralinguistic relata, and various other contextual factors such as the occasion of use, speaker's intent, ostensive gestures, and so forth, that collectively fix a definite spatial and temporal location of a certain employment of an expression-type and thereby indirectly pick out an expression-token of that type. So, for instance, the very same circumstance may be described either by saying: Smith is the referent of the expression-token "my friend here" (which token emerged from Jones's mouth while he was gesticulating in a certain manner at 3:00 p.m., August 5, 1988, at the end of the Newport Pier), or by saying: Jones used the expression-type "my friend here" in conjunction with a certain gesture at 3:00 p.m., August 5, 1988, at the end of the

Newport Pier, to refer to Smith, even though the first describes a two-place relation between token and referent, and the second a six-place relation among an expression-type, a referent, a speaker, a gesture, a place, and a time.

Now, if Aristotle's semantical apparatus contained the distinction between context-independent and context-dependent relations, he could dispose of sentences like (1), (3), and (4) without much trouble. He could, for example, explain the truth of (1) by first noting that the expression-type *white,* when it occurs as subject in a true token of that sentence, does not refer to its own usual denotation, which is of course the nonsubstantial entity whiteness, but rather to some particular (primary) substance, and then explaining the truth of that token as due to the fact that the substance so referred to is in fact a man.

It is quite apparent, however, that Aristotle does not have this distinction available to him either in the *Categories* or in the *Posterior Analytics.* The sole semantical relation he recognizes in these works is the signification relation, and this, without a doubt, is context-independent.[3] According to the semantics of *Categories* 4, the expression *white* therefore can stand in only one semantical relation: it signifies the nonsubstantial quality whiteness and nothing else, it signifies it once and for all, and in a way that is independent of features of any particular occasions of its use.

But even though Aristotle does not have the conceptual gear necessary to perform modern treatments of sentences like (1), (3), and (4), he puts what resources he does possess to ingenious use in explaining their truth. This explanation, which is accomplished solely in terms of the context-independent signification relation and the categorial scheme, is perhaps most explicit in the *Metaphysics* Γ passage where he treats sentences (3) and (4): "I say, for instance, that 'The white is cultured,' and 'The cultured is white' [are true] because both [whiteness and cultured] are accidents of a man" (1007b4–5). Here we have in effect an existentially quantified statement of the truth conditions for (3) and (4), which may be generalized to all intercategorial predications whose grammatical subjects and predicates are both nonsubstantial:

> If 'A is B' is true (where 'A' signifies A, 'B' signifies B,
> and A and B are both in nonsubstantial categories),
> there exists a primary substance S such that A and B
> both belong per accidens to S.[4]

But sentences like (3) and (4) are not the only type of true intercategorial predication that were seen to have no place in S_0. There are also sentences like (1), whose subject signifies a nonsubstance but whose predicate signifies a secondary substance, recognized at *Posterior Analytics* 81b24. Hence, the solution found in *Metaphysics* Γ can be generalized further so that it includes these and provides truth conditions for all intercategorial predication with nonsubstantial subjects no matter what the categorial status of their predicates:

> If 'A is B' is true (where 'A' signifies A, 'B' signifies B,
> and A is not a substance), there is a primary substance
> S such that A belongs per accidens to S, and B belongs
> (either per se or per accidens) to S.

I suggest that it is this general treatment of such sentences that Aristotle is recommending, albeit in overly terse language, when he says at *Posterior Analytics* 81b24 that the reason (1) is true is simply that whiteness is an accident of the man.

With this understanding of Aristotle's method of dealing with these sentences in mind, we are now in a suitable position to address two disturbing little puzzles concerning his discussion of per se and per accidens predication in *Posterior Analytics* 1.4. The first of these is actually something of an anomaly: the passage where Aristotle discusses his third sense of *per se* and *per accidens* does not fit well with its surrounding context. Each of the other senses of these terms discussed in *Posterior Analytics* 1.4 properly apply to sort of predication (or predicative relation), which is in keeping with the general aim of the chapter to specify the requisite features of scientific premises. Yet, as Aristotle explicates the third sense of these terms, they apply not to sentences but to terms, or what I have called in chapter 3 sentential elements. To say the least, it would be peculiar for a systematic writer like Aristotle in the middle of a protracted discussion about predications suddenly to switch tracks for three lines and concern himself with another subject and then to switch back again without the slightest warning.[5] Furthermore, there is no other location in the *Organon* where the terms *per se* and *per accidens* are used to apply to terms rather than connections between terms.

The other puzzle concerns the interpretation of Aristotle's remarks at *Posterior Analytics* 81b24. He says there that sentence (1) is a case of per accidens predication, yet an examination of his discussion earlier at 73a35–b16 seems to indicate that this sentence does not fit neatly into any of the three types of per accidens (namely, types 1, 2, and 4) explicitly discussed there. Evidently, he must think that there is another type of per accidens predication besides these three. But how is the omission of any mention of this further type to be explained? Should we say that it is a simple oversight, and that he simply forgot to include this type in his list in Chapter 4, even though its existence is clearly recognized in Chapter 19? Or should we say that Aristotle didn't discover the new type until he wrote Chapter 19, and for reasons now hidden from us was unwilling or unable to revise the list he had already drafted? Or should we blame the omission on his ancient editors?

Such explanations, being more on the order of biography and psychology than history of philosophy, are, for lack of discoverable criteria of correctness, inherently unsatisfying. They should be supplanted wherever possible by more detached accounts that aim at making sense of the text as it stands without the aid of such speculative hypotheses. In the present case, I shall offer an account that dissolves the appearance of strain between 73a35–b16 and 81b24–7 while at the same time accounting for what appears to be an anomalous introduction of the third sense of *per se* and *per accidens* at 73b6–8.

The key to this account is contained in the single insight that at 73b6–8, just as in the passages immediately surrounding it, Aristotle is primarily concerned with a certain type of predication, despite his superficial interest there in terms. What is more, the type of per accidens predication he discusses there is precisely the type he represents by (1) at 81b24, and also by (3) and (4) at *Metaphysics* 1007b4–5. In order to see exactly how these passages are related, it may first be noted that the two terms which Aristotle labels "per accidens" at 73b6–8, τὸ βαδίζον and τὸ λευκὸν, are both nominal phrases formed with a neuter singular adjectival form signifying a nonsubstance and a matching article. Such expressions, as we noticed above, are exactly the type whose occurrence as subjects characterizes sentences like (1), (3), and (4). In fact, the second of the two *is* the subject of sentences (1) and (3).

Now at 73b6 Aristotle gives as the reason that some terms are per se that they are "not said of anything else as subject" (μὴ καθ'ὑποκειμένου λέγεται ἄλλου τινός), and from this it may be inferred that he thinks τὸ βαδίζον and τὸ λευκὸν are per accidens precisely because they (or more accurately, their significata) *are* said of something else as subject. But what exactly does this mean? It is important not to be misled here by the unfortunate intrusion of *Categories* terminology, for here the expression "said of" is evidently used with a meaning different from what it has in the *Categories*. Here it refers not to what we called in chapter 3 the "said-of" relation, but to inherence, the very relation it is contrasted with in the *Categories*. This can be seen clearly in Aristotle's choice of examples. At 73b7 he gives as an example of something being "said of something else as subject" the case of something (presumably an animal) walking, and in the *Categories* scheme this is patently not a case of the said-of relation, but of inherence. Furthermore, the characterization given in the same place of terms that are per se (that is, whose significata are *not* said of anything else as subject) is "substance and such terms as signify particulars" (ἡ δ'οὐσία καὶ ὅσα τόδε τι σημαίνει). Apparently, the former are secondary substance-terms such as *man* and *horse,* and the latter are proper names of particular substances, such as *Socrates.* Now since the significata of such terms, being in Substance, are precluded by (S7) from inhering in anything, these examples reinforce the view that the expression "said of" at *Posterior Analytics* 73b6 refers not to the said-of relation of the *Categories* but to the inherence relation instead.

So Aristotle's explicit point, which pertains to terms, is that expressions like τὸ βαδίζον and τὸ λευκὸν are per accidens because their significata inhere in something else. Now comes the crucial step. At *Metaphysics* 1007b4–5 (and with less clarity at *Posterior Analytics* 81b24–7) Aristotle makes precisely the same point about the very same expressions, and he does so in language that is nearly identical (except that he replaces the misleading expression "said of" with the more perspicuous phrase "is an accident of"). However, in the *Metaphysics* passage (and in *Posterior Analytics* 1.19), Aristotle is no longer talking about such terms in isolation, as he does in *Posterior Analytics* 1.4, but rather as they occur as subjects in such per accidens predication as (1), (3), and (4). It is therefore reasonable to surmise that Aristotle's grounds for classifying these predications as per accidens is that their subject terms are per accidens in the sense expounded at 73b6–8, and that the sense of *per accidens* employed at *Metaphysics* 1007b4–5 and *Posterior Analytics* 81b24 is derivative of that sense. Hence, while the superficial point of 73b6–8 is again that certain terms are per accidens, the important submerged point that connects this passage with its surrounding context is that *predications* having such terms as subjects are consequently themselves per accidens (in a derivative sense), and hence do not qualify as scientific premises.

I said at the beginning of this discussion that according to the interpretation of *Posterior Analytics* 73b6–8 I am defending, Aristotle's main concern in that passage is not with a type of per se predication, but with a type of per accidens predication. Now a stronger point can be put: it ap-

pears that there is no independent class of type 3 per se predications identified in *Posterior Analytics* 1.4. If there were, then since Aristotle holds
that *per se* and *per accidens* are complementary in meaning, this would
mean that all that is needed to count a sentence as type 3 per se is that it
not be an intercategorial predication with a nonsubstantial subject. Even
if we assume that 73b6–8 is concerned exclusively with sentences whose
subjects, no matter what the category of their significata, *refer* to substances (though I have argued that Aristotle himself has no way of making
this distinction), that would still leave the class of type 3 per se predications so wide as to include both per se and per accidens predication of all
of the other types.

Now since, as we saw at the beginning of chapter 4, the overall purpose of the discussion of per se predication in *Posterior Analytics* 1.4 is to
identify a group of sentences that are suitable scientific premises (provided they are also κατὰ παντός and ᾗ αὐτό), it would seem that if Aristotle recognizes a class of type 3 per se predications, he would be giving
them this elevated status. It is hardly likely, however, that his intention is
to make such obviously contingent sentences as

(5) Socrates is white,

which he categorizes as per accidens in all other senses of that term, into
suitable candidates for scientific premises. A much more plausible view,
in light of the fact that 73b6–8 is concerned explicitly with terms, and
only indirectly with sentences, is that Aristotle there recognizes no independent classification of per se predications parallel to the sense of *per
accidens* he employs at *Posterior Analytics* 81b24 and *Metaphysics*
1007b4. Hence, there is an important difference in emphasis between
73b6–8 and its surrounding passages. While in each of those other passages Aristotle is concerned to characterize a type of per se predication to
include in his theory of science, here his concern is solely to identify a
certain type of per accidens predication he wishes to exclude.

DEMONSTRATION AND CAUSAL CONNECTIONS

According to the *Categories* semantics, and (S5) in particular, there are
only two types of true predication: those that express instances of the
said-of relation, and those that express inherence relations. Now Aristotle's remarks at *De Interpretatione* 9.18b5ff. make it clear that he
thinks many typical examples of inherence-sentences, if not all of them,

are fortuitously true, that is, true by virtue of the operations of "chance" (ἡ τύχή). There he cites as an undesirable feature of a doctrine under consideration its consequence that the truth of predications that veridically attribute (or deny) the predicate "(is) white" to "particular things" (presumably primary substances) would be a matter of necessity. This, he declares, in turn implies that nothing comes about from chance, a consequence he evidently takes to be false. Clearly, this reasoning relies on the assumption that such predications, which we saw in chapter 3 to be among Aristotle's favorite examples of inherence-sentences, are also paradigmatic examples of sentences he thinks are fortuitously true. This is why he can so readily endorse the conditional that if *they* aren't fortuitous then no predications are.

Further, since Aristotle here and elsewhere contrasts what comes about "from chance" (ἀπὸ τύχῆς) with what comes about "out of necessity" (ἐξ ἀνάγκης)[6] and since we have already seen that he makes the latter condition a requirement for scientific premises, we should expect he would not allow fortuitous truths to function in demonstrations. And indeed, he explicitly denies both that there can be scientific knowledge of such truths, and that they can occur, in demonstrative syllogisms in *Posterior Analytics* 1.30, and in somewhat more obscure language at *Prior Analytics* 1.13. 32b18. These passages prompt the view that the only type of true predications recognized in *Categories* that would be appropriate for demonstrations in the *Analytics* are those expressing the said-of relation.[7]

For all this, there are two very compelling reasons for thinking that the simple twofold division of predications in the *Categories* is inadequate for isolating the scientific propositions with which Aristotle is concerned in the *Posterior Analytics*. For as we noticed earlier, he argues at considerable length in *Posterior Analytics* 2.3–10 (especially at 90b28–91a12) that propositions that are true as a matter of definition cannot, except in a distended sense, be the objects or products of demonstration.[8] In restating this view at 93b16 after having just argued for it, Aristotle makes it clear that the reason such statements are not demonstrable in the strict sense is that they cannot function as conclusions of demonstrative syllogisms. But since he sees all type 1 per se predications as definitionally true, and since there is no recognition in the *Categories* of any other nonfortuitous truths besides type 1 per se predications, it appears that if Aristotle were to stick with the crude division of the *Categories*, the class of statements that could function as conclusions in demonstrations in the *Posterior Analytics* would effectively be empty.

But of course we already know that Aristotle does not confine himself to the crude *Categories* division of predications when he comes to outline his theory of demonstration in the *Posterior Analytics*. In fact, what has already been noticed about his more refined semantical views in the *Analytics* implies a partial solution to the problem just formulated. We saw in chapter 5 that he recognizes in the *Posterior Analytics* an additional class of nonfortuitous truths besides type 1 per se predications, namely type 2 per se predications, which connect a divided genus to its dividing differentiae. But even with the class of scientific propositions enlarged to include both types 1 and 2 per se predications, that still leaves the subject matter of Aristotelian science severely restricted to what we might now call analytic truths. This is because the truth of both these sorts of per se predication is insured by the network of what-is-it relations that were seen in chapter 3 to underlie the doctrine of the categories. Thus, a division that limits the interests of science exclusively to such definitional truths consigns to the operations of chance the whole range of predications whose truth is not so insured.

From the standpoint of modern philosophers of science, a theory of scientific explanation that took such a narrow view of the scientific domain would be utterly intolerable, since it would exclude precisely the sort of statement with which scientists are most concerned: those logically contingent, but highly probable, generalizations thought to express natural causal connections. Indeed, the only kind of premise countenanced by such a theory, those whose truth follows from the definitions of the terms they contain, are the concerns of such exact disciplines as mathematics and logic, which are generally classified as sciences only in a very special sense of that term.

To be sure, Aristotle's displeasure with any wholesale exclusion of nonanalytic truths from the compass of science would not be so acute as this, since his numerous mathematical examples of scientific reasoning throughout the first book of the *Posterior Analytics* indicate that he regards the mathematical disciplines as important, and perhaps even paradigmatic, sciences.[9] On the other hand, it is equally evident, both from his frequent use of nonmathematical examples of scientific reasoning in Book 2 and from the directions of his own scientific interests that he intends his theory to cover not just the derivation of mathematical propositions but also the explanation of highly probable propositions of natural science that one cannot reasonably disregard as merely fortuitous. In fact, I shall now go on to argue that the latter do in fact make up an important subclass of Aristotelian per se predications.

POSTERIOR ANALYTICS 73b10–16:
TYPE 4 PER SE PREDICATION

"X happens per se$_4$ to Y if X happens to Y in virtue of [Y] itself. Example: Death happens to a slaughtered thing in virtue of 'the slaughtered' itself [that is, in virtue of a thing's being slaughtered], so death happens per se$_4$ to a slaughtered thing." It must be admitted to begin with that this explication by itself does very little to illuminate the character of the sort of predication under discussion. All it says is that X happens to Y per se$_4$ just in case X happens to Y "in virtue of [Y] itself" (δι'αὐτό). But since, so far as H. Bonitz has discerned,[10] there is little if any difference in meaning between the Aristotelian expressions δι'αὐτό (because of itself) and καθ'αὑτό (per se), and since the meanings of both these expressions are in any case equally obscure, this explication is not likely to contribute much to our understanding of Aristotle's use of *per se*.

However, as so often happens in cases where his theoretical remarks leave residual perplexity, Aristotle's propitious insertion of an illuminating example in this passage enables us to get through to his intended meaning. Although he doesn't actually display a type 4 per se predication at 73b10–16, what he does say there leaves little question that he thinks the following fits the bill:

> (6) Death happens to some slaughtered [thing] (τι σφαττόμενον).

However, it is not the example itself but the explanation of its truth offered at b15 that provides the key to understanding Aristotle's use of δι'αὐτό, and ultimately to understanding the nature of his type 4 per se predications. The reason that (6) is a type 4 per se truth, he says, is that an animal does not only die when it is slaughtered; it also dies *because* it is slaughtered. As my emphasis suggests, the crucial expression in this explanation is the word "because," which translates the Greek διά. Now it is well known to modern philosophical logicians that "because" constructions can be used to express a vast spectrum of connections ranging from entailment (or logical consequence) among propositions to the tenuous connection between an all but capricious act and a whim that precedes it. Moreover, an exactly analogous elasticity has recently been observed in the ancient usage of διά.[11]

What type of connection, then, does Aristotle mean to express by his use of this preposition at 73b15? There are two initially plausible answers

to this question, each of which can be seen to follow from a corresponding way of understanding the verb σφάζειν (to slaughter), whose passive
finite and infinitive forms both occur in Aristotle's explanation of the
truth of (6). If the verb is taken to mean something like "to kill a captive
animal," "to kill in a certain manner, or with a certain kind of instru-
ment," or otherwise to involve definitionally the notion of putting the object of the verb to death, then the διά at b15 would seem to be a logical
"because" (that is, would seem to indicate the specification of a logically
sufficient condition for death). If, on the other hand, σφάζειν is understood, as it is by G. R. G. Mure in the Oxford translation,[12] simply to refer in a minimal sense to the immediate acts of slaughter, for instance, the
cutting of the throat, then the "because" at b15 should be read with
weaker force to indicate a causal relation between an animal's undergo-
ing that physical operation and its subsequent death.

DEMONSTRATION AND
"FOR-THE-MOST-PART" PREDICATIONS

Since both of these meanings of σφάζειν are well within the range of the
actual ancient usage of that term, how are we to decide between what
appear to be two equally plausible interpretations? The way out of this
quandary is again to be found in Aristotle's remarkable knack for providing just the right example at just the right time. In this case his choice of
examples constitutes strong evidence that the class of type 4 per se predications discussed at *Posterior Analytics* 73b10–16 is meant to include a
type of statement he elsewhere describes as "generally true," or "true for
the most part" (ἐπὶ τὸ πολύ). And since I shall also argue that these last
are patently the type of causal generalizations Aristotle includes within
the scope of his theory of demonstration, this will support the causal interpretation of sentence (6).

It must first be noticed that Aristotle's ἐπὶ τὸ πολύ predications typically have very general subjects, that is, subjects that apply to a great
many cases.[13] What he evidently means when he says that such a sentence
is "true for the most part" is that its predicate applies to most (or more
plausibly, a preponderance) of the cases to which its subject applies. So,
for instance, when he says at *Posterior Analytics* 96a10 that even though
it is not "always" (ἀεί) the case that a man grows chin whiskers, it is
nonetheless generally true that he does, Aristotle is asserting that most (or
by far most) men do have whiskers, even though some do not.

The distinctly quantitative nature of the expression ἐπὶ τὸ πολύ can make it seem initially plausible that in singling out this type of predication Aristotle is simply pointing to the purely statistical fact that there are some instances of high but imperfect correlation between event-types in the natural universe. But this statistical view of ἐπὶ τὸ πολύ predication is easily dispelled by the observation that there is a conspicuous absence of examples of predications expressing correlations that could be called purely coincidental. Any reasonably perceptive observer—and Aristotle certainly was that—would certainly be aware of some freak statistical regularities due to nothing but chance, such as every member of a certain dinner party being born in the same month. Yet virtually every one of his actual examples of ἐπὶ τὸ πολύ predication falls cleanly within the class of what we would now identify as causal generalizations (for example, *Prior Analytics* 1.13.32b7; *Posterior Analytics* 2.12.96a10; *Metaphysics* 6.2.1026b34).

The absence of examples of purely statistical regularities might be explained by the hypothesis that Aristotle simply does not recognize their practical possibility, but only if it could be established that he requires a relatively high level of generality for the *subject terms* of ἐπὶ τὸ πολύ statements. For certainly, as the number of cases examined becomes larger the actual statistical frequencies of events converge upon their theoretical probabilities. So if it could be shown that Aristotle insists every ἐπὶ τὸ πολύ predication must have a subject that is extremely general, and that he regards the threshold of ἐπὶ τὸ πολύ truth as quite high, then it might be possible to argue that the ἐπὶ τὸ πολύ classification really is statistical in nature and he simply denies the practical possibility of there being any freak correlation of a sufficiently high degree to pass the threshold. However, to my knowledge Aristotle never says or implies that there is any minimum generality requirement on the subject terms of ἐπὶ τὸ πολύ predications. Hence, if what he has in mind is just a statistical category, then it is hard to see how he could fail to notice that there are some general (though, of course, not very general) sentences whose truth is purely a matter of coincidence.

In any case, there is evidence that his restriction of examples to causal truths is not due simply to a lack of imagination on Aristotle's part. He repeatedly contrasts what is ἐπὶ τὸ πολύ with what "comes about from chance" (ἀπὸ τύχης), both directly (*De Generatione et Corruptione* 2.6.333b7; *De Caelo* 2.8.283a33; *Posterior Analytics* 1.30.87b19; *Eudemian Ethics* 14.1247a32; *Problemata* 91b31) and indirectly, by equating what is ἐπὶ τὸ πολύ with what is true "by nature" (κατὰ φυσίν; *De Gen. Animalium* 4.8.777a19−21), and by contrasting the latter with fortuitous occurrences (*Metaphysics* 7.7.1032a12; 12.3.1070a6; *De Part. Animalium* 1.1.641b22). This contrast indicates that he consciously discounts the possibility of coincidental general truths, and that he therefore regards the truth of all ἐπὶ τὸ πολύ statements as due to the operations of nature. As such, their character is very much like that of general truths now regarded as expressing causal connections.

If it is now granted that ἐπὶ τὸ πολύ statements express causal connections, and that Aristotle therefore has good theoretical reason to include them in the class of scientific premises and conclusions, we have next to discover whether he actually does so in *Posterior Analytics* 1.4. Here we should notice first that the doctrine of ἐπὶ τὸ πολύ predication is present virtually throughout the *Corpus,* the only significant exception being the *Categories,* which was already seen to adhere to the crude twofold division of predications reflected in (S5). In fact, it is found in such works as *De Interpretatione* (19a21) and *Prior Analytics* (32b7) that are quite early, even on the most conservative chronological orderings of Aristotle's works. Moreover, there are at least three good reasons for thinking that Aristotle consistently regards such statements as scientifically respectable. To begin with, he often sets them in the middle position of a threefold classification, contrasting them on one side with necessary truths (that is, types 1 and 2 per se predication and a certain type of propria predication to be discussed shortly), which he says are "always [true]" (ἀεί),[14] and on the other side with (genuine) accidental predications that he says can express connections that "can happen in one way or another" (ὁ καὶ οὕτως καὶ μὴ οὕτως δυνατόν; *Prior Analytics* 32b12). Whenever he makes this threefold division, he invariably insists that only the first two types (necessary predications and ἐπὶ τὸ πολύ predications) can be studied by science (*Posterior Analytics* 1.30.87b19–28; *Metaphysics* 6.2.1027a16–29).

Secondly, many of the examples of syllogistic demonstration he gives in *Posterior Analytics* 2 involve connections that evidently hold only for the most part, (for instance, that international aggressors become involved in war [11.94a37–69], that postprandial walks aid digestion [b9–19[15]], and that longevity is due to dry constitution in birds and to the absence of a gall bladder in quadrupeds [17.99b5–7]), and this is confirmed when he explicitly describes many of the actual conclusions he generates in his scientific treatises as ἐπὶ τὸ πολύ (for example, *De Generatione Animalium* 1.19.727b29; 4.4.770b9–13, 8.777a19–21). And finally, in the *Analytics* passages (discussed above in chapter 1) where he describes his recommended procedure for selecting demonstrative premises by Aristotelian division, he clearly admits the possibility of finding and using ἐπὶ τὸ πολύ premises. In particular, at *Posterior Analytics* 2.12.96a16–17 he merely insists that the immediate premises of ἐπὶ τὸ πολύ conclusions must themselves be ἐπὶ τὸ πολύ, and at *Prior Analytics* 1.27.43b33–37 he makes the same point, and says that for this reason it is necessary, in the process of collecting syllogistic premises, to identify those terms that follow "for the most part," or are "for the most part" followed upon by, a given subject.

Yet despite Aristotle's apparently fixed view that ἐπὶ τὸ πολύ connections belong within the field of scientific inquiry, he seems to ignore them in *Posterior Analytics* 1.4, the very chapter where he explicitly identifies the statements that can function as demonstrative premises and conclusions. The explanation for this apparent omission, I suggest, is that it is only apparent; ἐπὶ τὸ πολύ predications are discussed in that chapter, though under the heading of type 4 per se predications. The main evidence for this view, as I indicated above, is derived primarily from Aristotle's choice of examples. We noted earlier that on one plausible interpretation of Aristotle's explanation of the truth of sentence (6), Death happens to some slaughtered [thing] (τι σφαττόμενον), which is his lone example of a type 4 per se predication, the sentence can be read as expressing a causal relation between the two event-types mentioned in it. An examination of examples of ἐπὶ τὸ πολύ predications elsewhere shows them to be of exactly the same type: general statements expressing causal connections between event-types. Among those examples are:

> (7) A man becomes gray-haired [as he ages]. (*Prior Analytics* 1.13.32b7)
>
> (8) A man grows chin whiskers [as he ages]. (*Posterior Analytics* 96a10)
>
> (9) The weather is hot in the dog days [of August]. (*Metaphysics* 1026b34)

The similarity between these examples and (6), together with the fact that Aristotle has reason to make ἐπὶ τὸ πολύ respectable, provide good grounds for reading his explanation of the truth of (6) in a causal manner and for assimilating ἐπὶ τὸ πολύ predications into his type 4 per se classification. This assimilation is given further support by the even more striking similarity between the accidental predication Aristotle contrasts with sentence (7) at *Prior Analytics* 1.13.32b13:

> (10) An earthquake happens while an animal is walking,

and the example he gives of type 4 per accidens predication at *Posterior Analytics* 73b16:

> (11) The sky lightens while something walks.

DEMONSTRATION AND *PER SE PROPRIA*

This interpretative matter is complicated by the fact that there is another type of statement that seems to be quite unlike ἐπὶ τὸ πολύ truths but that Aristotle evidently also places under the heading of type 4 per se predication. These are sentences that attribute to some subject a certain subtype of what he refers to as *"propria"* (ἴδια). Such predications receive their fullest treatment in the *Topics* (especially at 102a18, 120b23, and throughout Book 5), but they are mentioned by name in the *Posterior Analytics* at 73a7, and again at 96b26. What's more, Aristotle's most frequent example of a scientific explicandum in the latter work,

> (12) Triangles have [interior] angles equal to two right
> angles,

involves one of his favorite examples of an ἴδιον. According to Aristotle's intital introduction of propria at *Topics* 1.5.102a18, they are distinguished by two conditions: if one thing is a proprium of another, then the expression that signifies the first must not state anything in the essence, or "the what it was to be" (τὸ τί ἦν εἶναι)[16] of the second, and the first must belong only to the second. This second condition is then redescribed as the requirement that propria must be "convertible" with their subjects, which means that for every true proprium predication there is a corresponding true universal biconditional containing the same terms.

The example Aristotle provides in this passage shows clearly what he has in mind:

> (13) Man is capable of learning grammar.

Since none of the various definitions of man presented in the *Corpus* makes reference to the capacity mentioned in (13), and since (according to *Topics* 101b38) a definition states the τὸ τί ἦν εἶναι of its definiendum, we may assume that (13) does meet the first condition given at a18. Moreover, in Aristotle's own words, "if [a thing] is a man, it is capable of learning grammar, and if [a thing] is capable of learning grammar, then it is a man" (*Topics* 102a21–23). This is quite clearly what is meant by the second condition, since it simply means that the capacity for learning grammar belongs to all men and to men alone.[17]

Now, as Aristotle himself recognizes at *Topics* 5.1.128b15ff., these two conditions are so general that they can be satisfied by predications of vastly disparate characters, and only some of these he thinks to be of interest to science. In particular, these are predications that involve what he calls at 128b15 "per se propria" ($\kappa\alpha\theta'\alpha\dot{\upsilon}\tau\acute{o}$ $\ddot{\iota}\delta\iota\alpha$), where even though the proprium in question is not in the "what it was to be" of the subject (as is dictated by the first condition on propria), there is nonetheless some conceptual connection between subject and predicate that accounts for the truth (indeed, the necessary truth) of the sentence. Clearly, sentence (13) is of this type, since although grammatical capacity is not mentioned in the definition of man, there is an obvious conceptual connection between something being a man and it being able to learn grammar.[18]

There can be no question that these predications of per se propria make up an important group of propositions of Aristotelian science. They are especially important to the mathematical sciences such as geometry or arithmetic, where the aim is to demonstrate the truth of certain necessary (as opposed to merely causal), but nondefinitional propositions from a set of given definitions and axioms. This again is evidenced by the fact that

(12) Triangles have [interior] angles equal to two right angles,

Aristotle's favorite example of a scientific demonstrandum in the *Posterior Analytics,* involves one of these per se propria. Since the definition of triangle contains no reference to interior angles, the predicate of this sentence cannot signify anything in the essence of its subject, and so (10) is not a definitional truth. Furthermore, there is very little doubt that Aristotle views this as a case of convertible predication. And since he is no doubt aware that the axioms, definitions, and postulates of geometry can be shown to entail that whatever is a triangle possesses the property mentioned in (12), he would certainly classify that property as a per se proprium.

On the other hand, Aristotle also explicitly recognizes that there are other true predications besides those that ascribe per se propria, which likewise satisfy the two general conditions on propria, but in which the connection between subject and predicate is entirely fortuitous.[19] For example, he indicates at *Topics* 129a3 that if a sentence such as

(14) Socrates is walking in the Agora,

were to be uttered at a time when Socrates was in fact the only pedestrian thing in the Agora, it would have to be regarded as involving the attribution of a proprium, albeit a temporary one. And this is as it should be, since on such an occasion (14) would plainly satisfy both conditions for propria predications given at 102a18. For walking in the Agora is certainly no part of the essence of Socrates, yet on that occasion he is precisely the extension of the predicate of (14). But even though this sentence is strictly speaking a proprium predication, Aristotle maintains throughout the *Corpus* that something's walking or being in a certain place are the kind of genuinely accidental states of affairs that hold no scientific interest. Hence, such accidental sentences as (14) should quite naturally be absent from the theory of demonstrative knowledge outlined in the *Analytics*.

By contrast, there is ample evidence that necessary predications of propria of the per se variety are supposed to figure importantly in Aristotle's theory. Besides the fact noted earlier that the mathematical proprium mentioned in (12) is the most frequently cited example in the *Posterior Analytics* of a per se attribute whose existence can and should be demonstrated, there is also a host of programmatic passages from both *Analytics* leading to essentially the same conclusion. For instance, at *Posterior Analytics* 2.13.96b15–26, the passage in which Aristotle explains how his version of the method of division can prove useful in undertaking the systematic study of a genus,[20] he says that one should try, among other things, to discover the "proper affections" (ἴδια πάθη) of one's subject.[21] Likewise, in *Prior Analytics* 1.27, whose concerns I have argued (in chapter 1) are closely parallel to those of *Posterior Analytics* 2.13, he makes much the same point in almost the same words: "We must differentiate among the consequents [of a given subject] those which are in the what-is-it, those which are predicated as 'propria' (ἴδια), and those which are predicated as [merely] accidentally" (*Prior Analytics* 43b7–12). For presumably, if it is his intention all along simply to collapse all propria into accidental attributes for scientific purposes, there would be no point in distinguishing the second and third classifications mentioned here.

Furthermore, a biological example supplied by Aristotle in *Posterior Analytics* 2.14 gives a pretty clear idea of exactly how propria will figure in the construction of demonstrative syllogisms once a subject-genus has been systematized according to the guidelines set out in the previous chapter. At 98a17–20, he indicates that it would be reasonable to proceed by first identifying certain characteristics of animals that always accompany possession of horns, such as having a third stomach or having a single row of teeth, and then arguing (syllogistically) that any subtype of horned animals must necessarily display these same characteristics. Now if, as seems plausible, we take this as a description of an approved form of demonstration, and also assume that the attributes in question are necessary ἴδια of *horned animal,* we can understand Aristotle here as certifying demonstrations such as the following:

(i) All cows are horned, and
(ii) all (and only) horned animals have a third stomach,
    so
(iii) all cows have a third stomach,

where what is being demonstrated is that a per se proprium of a certain kind is also a necessary attribute (though not of course a proprium) of one of its subkinds. This then has far-reaching and important consequences for the account of the structure of demonstration given in part 1. For since the primary (affirmative) demonstrative premises considered in chapter 1 were limited to statements that are immediate but *not* convertible, the only sort of demonstrative syllogism in Barbara represented there:

(i) All B is A, and
(ii) all C is B, so
(iii) all C is A,

was a type in which the relations among its contained terms may be represented by the following vertical schema:

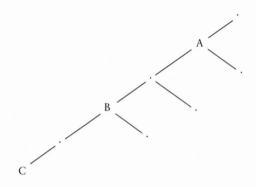

However, in light of the example at 98 a17–20, we can now see that in addition to this entirely vertical type of demonstration, Aristotle also recognizes the possibility of another sort, in which the terms of Barbara are related as follows:

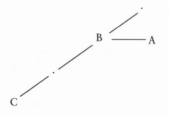

where the lateral connection between A and B is meant to represent the relation of mutual entailment (that is, convertibility) between a kind (B) and one of its per se propria (A). But now, this opens the further possibility of an *exclusively* lateral form of demonstration, represented by the schema,

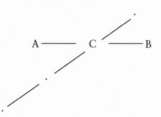

in which one explains the possession of one per se proprium (A) of a given kind (C) by reference to the possession of another of its per se propria (B). What is striking about this form of demonstration is that it accomplishes all of its explanatory work at a single divisional node. As applied to Aristotle's example at 98a17–20, this might involve, say, explaining the presence of a third stomach in horned animals by means of dental configuration:

    (i)   All (and only) things with a single row of teeth have
          a third stomach, and
    (ii) all (and only) horned animals have a single row of
          teeth, so
    (iii) all (and only) horned animals have a third stomach.

or perhaps the dental configuration might be explained by means of the third stomach.[22]

It is apparently because of the obvious importance of such sentences to Aristotle's science, most especially to his mathematics, that Mure includes per se propria predications among the type 4 per se predications discussed at *Posterior Analytics* 73b10–16.[23] Although he does not make his reasons for doing so explicit, they are no doubt analogous to those given above in the case of ἐπὶ τὸ πολύ predications: since we have seen that such statements make up an important class of scientific propositions in the *Posterior Analytics,* Aristotle must have included them somewhere in his catalogue of scientifically appropriate statements in *Posterior Analytics* 1.4. Moreover, the fact that he actually uses the expression *per se* in the *Topics* to distinguish these necessary propria from other types provides additional grounds for thinking that they are discussed somewhere in *Posterior Analytics* 1.4. But since he makes it a characteristic feature of per se propria predications that they are not definitionally true, their inclusion in types 1 and 2 is ruled out, and this leaves type 4 as the only remotely plausible place where they could be included.

A UNIFIED ACCOUNT

At first sight, it is admittedly hard to believe that Aristotle could indiscriminately lump per se propria predications and ἐπὶ τὸ πολύ predications together under a single heading in view of the fact that they seem so obviously different in character. For it seems that any proprium predication, including those of the per se variety, must be strictly universal by virtue of the convertibility condition, whereas the lack of precisely this feature is what Aristotle uses to distinguish ἐπὶ τὸ πολύ predications from necessary truths. It seems incredible that Aristotle could identify these two disparate types as type 4 per se predication without so much as a word to indicate the differences between them.

Yet despite its incredibility, there seems no way of escaping this conclusion. Certainly, the arguments offered above to support Mure's inclusion of per se propria predications among type 4 per se predications carry great weight, and yet we have seen that there are analogous and equally good reasons for interpreting *Posterior Analytics* 73b10–16 as being concerned with ἐπὶ τὸ πολύ predications. In addition, the conflation of the two types is supported by the fact that there is an almost perfect parallel between the examples given of type 4 per accidens predication at 73b6–8, and the sentences contrasted with ἐπὶ τὸ πολύ predications at *Prior Analytics* 32b15. Moreover, there are reasons independent from what is going on at *Posterior Analytics* 73b10–16 for thinking that Aristotle doesn't distinguish between these two types of statement. Even though he recognizes both types as scientific, and discusses each as such separately (indeed, sometimes even in a single work; compare *Posterior Analytics* 73a7 with 87b20), there is not a single passage where he mentions both, or says anything to indicate that they are distinct types. In fact, to my knowledge, there is no place in the entire *Corpus* where these two obviously important types of scientific statements are set side by side.

Fortunately, a very plausible way of dealing with this difficulty is provided by Mario Mignucci (1981). On Mignucci's suggestion, it is not necessary to understand Aristotle at 73b10–16 as attempting to place two very different sorts of predication under a single heading, because he holds that behind every "for-the-most-part" predication there lurks a per se proprium, or to put it even more strongly, that any "for-the-most-part" predication is actually a disguised form of a predication that assigns a per se proprium to its subject. To see how this suggestion addresses the difficulty just described, consider again one of Aristotle's paradigms of ἐπὶ τὸ πολύ predication:

> (8) A man grows chin whiskers [as he ages]. (*Posterior Analytics* 96a10)

I have already argued that Aristotle doesn't interpret this as a mere statement of statistical frequency but rather understands it as expressing some sort of causal necessity between aging and the emergence of whiskers. However, a number of recent studies suggest that Aristotle's basic model for understanding causality is not as a relation between events (whether construed types or tokens), but rather as the operations of "causal powers" residing in the "natures" of the subject-substances in which the causal effects in question obtain.[24] On this understanding, we can understand the emergence of chin whiskers in particular as the exercise of some causal power, P, involved or contained in the nature of man. This is where Mignucci's suggestion comes into play. For it is now plausible to interpret Aristotle as holding that P is possessed by every single specimen of man without exception, and accordingly to describe those occasional specimens without whiskers not as lacking P, but as instances where P, though possessed, fails to be manifested. On this suggestion then, corresponding to the ἐπὶ τὸ πολύ truth of

> (8) A man grows chin whiskers [as he ages],

Aristotle also recognizes the more fundamental truth of some such sentence as

(8') Every man has P (which for the most part is mani-
    fested by the growth of chin whiskers at the appro-
    priate time).

What is more, even though this power might be regarded in some weaker
sense as essential to the kind *man*, Aristotle would certainly not see it as
in the what-is-it of that kind as that narrower notion was interpreted in
chapter 3. Therefore, on the additional assumption that the power to
grow chin whiskers is special to man,[25] it would follow that (8') predicates a per se proprium of its subject.[26]

Having now examined each sense of *per se* and *per accidens* explicated in *Posterior Analytics* 1.4 separately, we can take a final overview of
the whole complex doctrine by classifying the various kinds of true predication we have encountered in the last three chapters according to their
suitability to serve in demonstrations. Among those statements that can
occur as demonstrative premises, but not as demonstrative conclusions,
we have placed "definitional" predications,[27] that is, type 1 per se predications (which may either place their subjects in their superordinate genera or constitute "constructive" definitions); whereas among sentences
that can occur as demonstrative conclusions are both type 2 per se predications (predications of differentiae to subsets of their subjects), and type 4
per se predications (predications of per se propria, and also ἐπὶ τὸ πολύ
truths). On the other hand, the two types of predication that cannot have
any place in demonstrations are type 3 per accidens (that is, intercategorial predications with nonsubstantial subjects) and predications that
are not per accidens in that sense but are per accidens in all three other
senses of that term (that is, genuine inherence predications).

SEVEN

——

Demonstration and Negation

NEGATIVE PREDICATION IN DEMONSTRATION

When Aristotle says in Book 1, Chapter 14 of the *Posterior Analytics* that demonstration characteristically proceeds by first-figure syllogisms, he does not specify further that the preferred inferential form is limited to Barbara, the only purely affirmative mood with all universal premises. This is no oversight. He opens his very next chapter by declaring that the primary premises of demonstration are not limited to affirmative immediate predications, but include immediate *negative* predications as well.[1] Thus, at the very least it is clear that Celarent, the one wholly universal negative mood in the first figure,

> (i)   No Bs are A, but
> (ii) all Cs are B, so
> (iii) no Cs are A,

is admitted here as an acceptable form of syllogistic demonstration.

Nor should this really be surprising from either a philosophical or a historical standpoint. In the first place, since the initial, framing stage of demonstration has been represented in chapter 1 as a direct descendant of Platonic διαίρεσις, and the latter characteristically proceeds by the identification of finer and finer necessary exclusion relations among kinds, it is to be expected that the products of the Aristotelian adaptation of that method should correspondingly include universal negative premises, since these are what normally convey such exclusion relations. But quite apart from any consideration of the specifics of Aristotle's theory, it also seems quite unlikely on general principles that a theory lacking the resources of negative predication would have much to recommend it as a comprehensive account of scientific explanation. To borrow one of Aristotle's own biological examples, such a theory could not allow this as a legitimate explanation:

(i) Snakes are reptiles, and
(ii) no reptiles give milk, but
(iii) mammaries are for the sole purpose of holding milk, so
(iv) snakes have no mammaries (*Parts of Animals* 692a10–14)[2]

PLATO ON SEMANTIC FRAGMENTATION

But if Aristotle thus has theoretical need to include some negative predications as legitimate demonstrative premises, he also has good reason to be troubled by their presence. This is because he inherits from Plato an appreciation of certain considerations that seem, prima facie at least, to infect the very idea of negative predication with conceptual difficulty. Notice first that the method of division practiced in Plato's *Sophist*, *Statesman*, and *Philebus* presupposes the coherence of negative predication. At the very heart of the method stands a characteristic step in which the divider comes to apprehend that a "kind" (γένος) that might have appeared to be monolithic, or "sound" (ὑγιής), in fact has a "seam" (διπλόην or συχνήν), by which is metaphorically conveyed that there is some pair of differentiating properties or characteristics each of which is had by some, but not all, members of the kind under division.

However, there is at least one passage in the *Sophist* where Plato seems to see a potential problem with the use of negation in division.[3] This occurs at 225B–C, where he has the Stranger and Theaetetus agree that the art of "antilogic" is divided into two parts, one of which, eristic, is described as "technical" (ἔντεχνον; by which is presumably meant that it is governed by rules or guidelines) while the other, which is left nameless, is characterized only by the essentially privative adverbs "purposelessly" (εἰκῆ) and "nontechnically" (ἀτέχνως). It is the "nameless" part of this division that gets singled out for deprecatory comment by the

Stranger at B11–C4: "This must be posited as a kind, since our account has indeed discerned it as a distinct thing, but it did not receive a name from those who came before, nor is it worthy of getting one from us now."

If we can assume that Plato's own thought is expressed by Theaetetus's unchallenged diagnosis of this lack of nameworthiness at C5–6— "True [nontechnical antilogic does not deserve a name]. For it is divided into parts which are too small and diverse (κατὰ σμικρὰ γὰρ λίαν καὶ παντοδαπὰ διῄρηται)"—then it is reasonable to surmise that he sees this defect as rooted in the fact that the group of activities falling under the essentially negative terms εἰκῇ and ἀτέχνως are insufficiently like one another to count collectively as a genuine unity. Of course, what is conspicuously left unsaid is just why such excessive diversity should have failure of nameworthiness as a result. Therefore, if we are to understand Theaetetus's remark as at all responsive, it will be necessary to supply a link between observed symptom and profferred cause. I suggest that the best candidate for this role is a species of meaning deficiency I will call *semantic fragmentation*. According to this suggestion, Plato is drawing on the insight that even if a common term, say F, were somehow to become associated with a group of sufficiently disparate elements, say all and only the items presently on my desktop, this would not constitute a genuine instance of common predication. Presumably, this is because even someone who had surveyed every one of the Fs could not thereby be taken to have discovered anything about the nature of Fness—about what it is to be an F—for the simple reason that there is no uniform nature there to discover. Ex hypothesi, the field of Fs ranges across a multiplicity of diverse natures. Where this is so, Plato will say, the group in question may in fact receive a common name, but they do so undeservedly.

As the example contrived in the last paragraph illustrates, not all instances of semantic fragmentation are cases involving negative differentiae. However *Sophist* 225B–D does seem to constitute evidence of a recognition on Plato's part that at least one possible cause of semantic fragmentation (and so of failure of nameworthiness) does involve the improper use of negative differentiae in the process of division. Further corroboration for this view comes from *Statesman* 262A–263B, a passage remarkably parallel to *Sophist* 225B–C in which the Stranger complains to the young Socrates about the use of negative differentiae such as "non-Hellene" or "not–ten thousand" in making divisions:

> We must be careful lest we break off one small fragment of a class and then contrast it with all the important sections left behind . . .

[for instance, as when] seeking to divide the class of human beings into two, [we] divide them into Greeks and barbarians . . . ignoring the fact that [the latter] is an indefinite class made up of peoples who have no intercourse with each other, and speak different languages. Lumping all this non-Greek residue together, [those who try to divide this way] think it must constitute one real class because they have a common name, "barbarian," to attach to it. Take another example. Someone might think he was dividing numbers into true classes if he cut off the number ten thousand from all others and set it apart as one class. He might go on to invent a single name for whole of the rest of number, and then claim that because it possessed the invented common name, it was in fact the other true class of number: "number other than ten thousand." Surely it would be better and closer to the real structure of the Forms to make a central division of number into odd and even, and of humankind into male and female.[4]

ARISTOTLE ON SEMANTIC FRAGMENTATION

There are a number of Aristotelian discussions of negative predicates where he evidently concurs with Plato that the use of such expressions raises the spectre of semantic fragmentation. One of these is Aristotle's quick critical remark at *Metaphysics* A.990b14 that the Platonist's "One-over-Many" principle unhappily entails the existence of negative forms, which is then expanded in Alexander's paraphrase of the *Peri Ideon,* as follows: "For if someone were to propose [that there could be an idea of not-being (τοῦ μὴ εἶναι ἰδέα)], then there would be an idea of things that are 'non-homogenous' (ἀνομογενῶν) and 'utterly different' (πάντῃ διαφερόντων). Such would be a letter and a man, for all of these are *not-horse*."[5]

It also appears that Aristotle takes an even darker view than does Plato on the dangers inherent in the use of negative predicates. For there is good reason to believe that he regards this sort of semantic fragmentation, in its most vicious form, as leading into the "Meinongian" problem of admitting nonexistents into one's ontology. This much is at least hinted at in *De Interpretatione* 2: "Let [terms such as 'not-man'] be called *indefinite names* (ὄνομα ἀόριστον) because they apply to all manner of things, both existent and non-existent (ὄντος καὶ μὴ ὄντος)" (16a32–34).[6]

Now this clearly takes matters beyond what is found in the *Sophist.*

Nevertheless, such unmistakable parallels between these Platonic and Aristotelian passages make it practically certain that the two writers agree that semantic fragmentation is at least one of the difficulties that must be overcome by any satisfactory account of negative predication. For even though Plato and Aristotle both see semantic fragmentation as a potential hazard inherent in the use of negative predicates, there is no evidence that either of them is prepared to follow what well may have been Parmenides's own drastic recommendation, that terms constructed out of negative particles should be banished altogether. It rather appears that both writers recognize an important distinction between cases of negative predication that do exhibit semantic fragmentation and others that are quite innocent of this defect, and they both attempt to immunize their respective theories of predication against this danger.

THE ARISTOTELIAN SOLUTION:
THE COMPARTMENTALIZATION OF SCIENCE

In order to appreciate the nature of Aristotle's proposal to achieve this immunization, it will be helpful to consider first what he perceives as distinguishing the defective occurrences of negative predicates. As the example given above from Alexander (81.3–4) illustrates, Aristotle's view is that semantic fragmentation occurs specifically when some negative term, *not-F*, is used in such a way that it purportedly denotes the complement of the denotation of *F* within some insufficiently restricted background field. Thus, *not-horse* is said not to signify an "idea" (ἰδέα)—that is, not to pick out a genuine property—on the ground that the class of objects of which it is true (*everything* that is not a horse—the complement of the class of horses within the domain of existents of every sort) is so wide and diverse (that is, so fragmented) as to include such unlikely cohabitants as men and alphabetical letters.[7] Again, Aristotle's (and Plato's) objection to such uses, according to the present interpretation, is ultimately that the negative predicate in such contexts lacks definite meaning. The argument is that if there are virtually no limits on what can satisfy the predicate *not-horse,* then it does not appear that anything determinate could be attributed to a subject by applying that predicate to it. The point, then, is that Aristotle does not see semantic fragmentation as a problem attached to the use of negative terms per se, but rather as one limited to cases where such expressions are meant to signify underrestricted complements.[8]

But if this is seen as the fundamental problem with negative predicates, its most plausible solution requires no great amount of ingenuity: one has simply to make sure that underrestricted complements are not allowed to stand as significata of negative terms. Indeed, there are strong indications that Aristotle finds nothing whatever wrong with the application of negative terms when the background class is sufficiently restricted. For example, at *Posterior Analytics* A.5.73b23–24, he remarks, "the even is the not-odd *within number,* inasmuch as the one follows upon the other," which clearly suggests that he thinks the term *not-odd* does possess a determinate meaning (namely that of the positive term *even*) so long as its application is understood as restricted to the field of numbers, which form the subject-genus of arithmetic.

This passage shows that Aristotle has no objection to sufficiently restricted uses of negative predicates. By contrast, however, ascertaining his attitude toward their use in underrestricted contexts is a much more complicated matter. On one hand, he seems quite prepared in *De Interpretatione* 2 and 3 to admit what he calls "indefinite" (ἀόριστον) "nouns" and "verbs," such as *not-man* and *not-ill* into his theory of predication, even though, as we saw, he regards their extensions as ranging so far as to include nonexistents.[9] He even remarks at *De Interpretatione* 10.19a9, that an "indefinite" expression "somehow signifies a unity" (ἐν γάρ πως σημαίνει τὸ ἀόριστον), while insisting at the same place that such expressions do not strictly qualify as nouns and verbs.[10]

On the other hand, the passages from Alexander considered above strongly suggest that Aristotle sees expressions like *not-horse* as having such radically fragmented extensions that they could not possibly signify genuine unities or carry determinate meanings. In addition to this, his discussion of "far-fetched explanations" (τὰ καθ' ὑπερβολήν εἰρημένα) in *Posterior Analytics* 1.13 indirectly implies that he disallows the use of underrestricted negative predications in the construction of authentic (that is, genuinely explanatory) demonstrative syllogisms. The actual example given at 78b25–27 of a syllogism that violates this stricture is in the second-figure mood Camestres:

        (i) Every breather is animal, and

A   (ii) no wall is animal, so

        (iii) no wall is breather,

but the first-figure (perfect) syllogism to which that is reduced is in Celarent:

> B
> (i)   No animal is wall, and
> (ii) every breather is animal, so
> (iii) no breather is wall.

With this reduction, the gist of Aristotle's complaint at b30 that "the middle stands too far away" (τὸ πλέον ἀποστήσαντα τὸ μέσον) is that the negative connection (between animal and wall) expressed by B(i) (or its contraposition) is too remote to explain why walls do not breathe.[11] By parity of reasoning, however, it is likely that he would make exactly the same complaint about the following syllogism in Barbara containing negative predicates as opposed to negative predications,[12]

> C
> (i)   Every breather is animal, and
> (ii) every animal is not-wall, so
> (iii) every breather is not-wall,

which would be tantamount to declaring that the use of underrestricted negative predicates, such as that in C(ii) here, has no proper place in scientifically illuminating explanations.[13]

The central argument of chapter 4 was that when Aristotle undertakes to give an analysis of the necessity of the most important type of scientific premise (namely, type 1 per se predications) in *Posterior Analytics* 1.4, he finds it useful to move beyond the relatively broad categorial divisions given explicitly in *Categories* 4, and to think of each of the categories (in the way that is implicit in the single-question method for generating categories) as possessing an internal hierarchical structure of kinds and subkinds ordered by the what-is-it relation. Now we can see in addition that he exploits this same hierarchical conception in the *Posterior Analytics* to immunize his theory of scientific predication against the danger of semantic fragmentation. This is evidenced most clearly at 1.7.75a38−b6 where he says that every demonstration must pertain to a single "underlying genus" (τὸ γένος τὸ ὑποκείμενον), and that it is not possible to conduct a demonstration that crosses over from one genus to another.[14] Moreover, much the same point seems to motivate Aristotle's remark at 77a22−26 that because unrestricted instantiations of the Law of Excluded Middle are subject to semantic fragmentation, that law must always be applied "upon a genus" (ἐπὶ τοῦ γένους),[15] as well as his view at *Categories* 11.13b14−20 that direct contraries can only be meaningfully applied within a single genus.

Admittedly, there is some difficulty in ascertaining exactly what Aristotle means by *genus* in these and like passages. For with the possible exception of those rare occurrences (if any) in biological contexts where this term refers specifically (as in modern biology) to items on the penultimate level of division, it is generally applied by Aristotle as a correlative with the term *species* at any level of division whatever. Hence, the same item might be called a species when considered as a subdivision of a higher kind, but a genus when it is subjected itself to further division. But if there is no inherent maximum degree of generality required to qualify a kind as a legitimate genus, then it might be asked how Aristotle's insistence that every demonstrative science must pertain to a single genus is supposed to protect his theory from the threat of semantic fragmentation.

The very way in which this question is put gets things the wrong way around. As it has been represented above, the defect I am calling "semantic fragmentation" is a sort of indeterminacy in meaning that comes in degrees. So, for example, *not-horse* within the class of material objects will be more determinate than its completely unrestricted application, but less so than when it is restricted to, say, vertebrates. It thus appears that what Aristotle has in mind is a kind of threshold past which such indeterminacy becomes intolerably problematic. As I am interpreting him, Aristotle does not first decide independently how specific a scientific genus must be and then go on to use this limit as a safeguard against semantic fragmentation. Rather he reasons in the opposite direction by fixing the line of maximum generality allowable in a legitimate scientific genus as that past which the application of negative predicates precipitates semantic fragmentation and purported demonstrations become far-fetched. Thus, although Aristotle has no hard and fast answer to the question of how specific a scientific genus must be, he does provide a rule for generating an answer on a case-by-case basis: it must be narrow enough that all the terms, negative and positive, employed in demonstrations conducted within it have determinate meanings.

Notes

———

Unless otherwise specified, all translations herein are my own, although I have often borrowed from the Loeb Classical Library and Oxford translations when they seemed impossible to improve upon.

INTRODUCTION

1. See Ross (1949) and Barnes (1975). Hintikka (1972) promises a full-length study of Aristotelian demonstration, but that work has yet to appear.

2. It is not meant to suggest only that: on the other side of the double entendre, this is also a book about the relation between an Aristotelian demonstrative system and its ultimate epistemological "origins" (that is to say, starting points).

3. Compare Ferejohn (1980).

4. This understanding is confirmed to a large extent by *Posterior Analytics* 2.1 and 2.2, which make the point that providing a syllogistic demonstration of a previously known fact (that is, a τὸ ὅτι) is tantamount to elucidating that on account of which it obtains (its τὸ διότι); see especially 2.1.89b30–31; 2.2.89b35–90a5. Here I mean to oppose not only the view that the theory of demonstration is an attempt to formalize the proper methods of scientific inquiry, but also the currently popular position advocated in Barnes (1969) and (1981) that it is offered as a theory of scientific pedagogy that sets out the most effective means by which a finished science can be imparted to students. For criticisms of this latter position, cf. chapter 1, note 4.

5. According to this complex pattern, the term exhibits a peculiar three-way

ambiguity, on some occasions denoting the knowing faculty (δύναμις) of the soul, on others the occurrent condition or state a soul is in when it knows, and on yet others the items of information (pieces or parts of knowledge) that serve as the objects or products upon which the knowing faculty or state of knowledge is employed or directed. For a discussion of how this multiple equivocity of ἐπιστήμη is involved in Plato's views concerning the unity of the virtues in the Socratic dialogues, see Ferejohn (1984).

6. This general interpretation of the structure of Aristotelian demonstration was announced programmatically in Ferejohn (1982), part of which chapter 1 below rehearses. In fact, the present work as a whole is an attempt to redeem promises made in note 27 of that article.

7. Because I maintain that the theory of demonstration is essentially and importantly based on Aristotle's syllogistic, I do not share the view of some recent writers (most notably, Barnes [1981] and Smith [1982]) that certain (but not all) parts of the *Posterior Analytics* were composed prior to Aristotle's development of the full syllogistic theory in the *Prior Analytics*. Besides having a general suspicion that the construction of such patchwork interpretations without the benefit of nondoctrinal, or external evidence is excessively speculative, I see no compelling reason to resort to it in the present case until it is shown that there are insurmountable obstacles to understanding demonstration in the way Aristotle himself characterizes it, as a kind of syllogism (*Prior Analytics* 1.4.25b26–30, *Posterior Analytics* 71b7).

CHAPTER 1: DEMONSTRATION, DIVISION, AND THE SYLLOGISM

1. One feature of the *Posterior Analytics* often pointed to by its detractors is that Chapters 2 and 10 of Book 1 seem to go over much the same ground, making it look as if Aristotle or his editors simply threw together a mass of material on the same subject without much concern for orderly exposition. On the view I am proposing, in *Posterior Analytics* 1.2, and indeed throughout the first three chapters of the work, Aristotle is concerned with developing a set of epistemological conditions he believes any theory of justification (i.e., ἀπόδειξις in the nontechnical sense) must meet, whereas in *Posterior Analytics* 1.10 he is involved in presenting a specific theory he has designed to meet these requirements. This, of course, is not to deny that he could have that theory in mind in the earlier chapter, but only that he is not yet prepared at that point to expound it.

2. Smith (1986) and chapter 6 of Irwin (1988) contain different accounts of how Aristotle argues in *Posterior Analytics* 1.3 against various nonfoundationalist theories of justification; Smith also offers some interesting conjectures about who might actually have advocated such views.

3. Earlier in this century, this controversy was intertwined with a historical debate over the correct chronological ordering of the two *Analytics*. Solmsen (1929) argues on textual grounds for reversing the traditional ordering of these

works reflected in their post-Aristotelian titles. (Incidentally, these arguments are recalled and defended in modified form in Barnes [1981]). Believing that the mature theory of the syllogism was not yet devised when the *Posterior Analytics* was written, Solmsen is quite naturally inclined towards antisyllogisticism, although I find very little resemblance between his views and Barnes's "scientific pedagogy" interpretation (on which, see Introduction, note 4 and chapter 1, note 4). On the other side, Ross (1949) contains detailed replies to Solmsen's textual arguments (see pages 7–22), and also reflects a commitment to strict syllogisticism in its systematic conflation of "primary premises" ($\pi\rho\hat{\omega}\tau o\nu$ $\pi\rho o\tau\acute{a}\sigma\epsilon\iota\varsigma$) and "first principles" ($\grave{a}\rho\chi\alpha\acute{\iota}$) in the *Posterior Analytics*.

For reasons that will become clear later, there may not in fact be any perfect examples of strict syllogisticism in more recent work on the *Posterior Analytics*, though Hintikka (1972) is a reasonable approximation. If there are no actual examples, then the position outlined here may be thought of merely as representing a tendency (which Hintikka undoubtedly does display) to give syllogistic interpretations of Aristotelian $\grave{a}\rho\chi\alpha\acute{\iota}$ whenever possible. Some recent examples of antisyllogisticism are Barnes (1969) and (1981), and Smith (1982).

4. Since my aim here is to provide a positive account of Aristotle's theory of demonstration, I shall not be concerned to rehearse all my reasons for rejecting these two opposing positions. The following section does raise a number of problems with Hintikka's account, but those remarks are intended mostly to highlight certain exegetical problems which are subsequently dealt with more adequately within the two-stage interpretation advocated here. I regard antisyllogisticism as a prima facie implausible last resort whose most powerful case is the absence of a fully satisfactory syllogistic interpretation of demonstration. I will therefore not argue directly against it, but instead try to obviate resort to it by actually producing such an interpretation. Nonetheless, I believe the plausibility of Barnes's pedagogical version of the position is undermined successfully (if inadvertently) in Burnyeat (1981). As what he describes as a "corrective or caveat" to Barnes, Burnyeat observes that the pedagogical contexts that interest Aristotle in the *Posterior Analytics* are not those in which "a teacher [imparts] new knowledge to virgin minds" (118), but are more akin to "an advanced university course in mathematics or biology" wherein "the scientist aims to display and share his principled understanding of the field" (118). It seems to me that Burnyeat here seriously understates the extent of his disagreement with Barnes on this issue. For as he himself points out, a presentation offered in the context of such "advanced pedagogy" will be more "instructive" ($\delta\iota\delta\alpha\sigma\kappa\alpha\lambda\iota\kappa\acute{\eta}$) if it is more "explanatorily illuminating" (119). But since the sort of advanced scientific pedagogy Burnyeat envisages is therefore one that is epistemologically ideal (in the sense that it is stripped of any assumptions about the special epistemic predicament or limitations of the learner), its demands turn out to coincide perfectly with those of scientific explanation, impersonally construed. Consequently, I think Burnyeat's "corrective" really amounts to a thorough repudiation of Barnes's view.

5. See *Sophist* 218ff. and *Statesman* 258ff.

6. See Cherniss (1944).

7. Cherniss (1944) maintains (54–82) that the chief intended target of Aristotle's attacks on διαίρεσις is Plato's successor, Speusippus, who evidently did offer it as a self-sufficient method of proving the essence of some subject (an aim that is undermined in *Posterior Analytics* 2.3–10), and not Plato himself, who seemed to regard it more as a mnemonic device for apprehending relations among Forms (*Sophist* 253C–E).

8. Aristotle also complains in *Posterior Analytics* 2.5 that there is nothing in the method itself to ensure that the divisions it generates will all be natural and essential. Aristotle's attempt to avoid this sort of deficiency within his own system will be taken up at some length in Part 2, below.

9. Essentially the same point is made in *Posterior Analytics* 2.5 at 91b33–92a5.

10. To this Aristotle could have added that such inferences cannot even be syllogisms (let alone demonstrative syllogisms) because they also violate the stricture laid down both at *Prior Analytics* 1.1.24a16 and *Posterior Analytics* 1.2.72a9 that syllogistic premises always involve *one* term being predicated of one other term. For (2), (3), (5), and (6) are all statements in which the disjunction of two terms is predicated of some third term. Incidentally, this same observation will be seen in chapter 5 to provide a significant reason for rejecting Barnes's proposal to interpret an important subclass of Aristotle's demonstrative premises (namely, the subtype of per se predications discussed at *Posterior Analytics* 1.4.73a35–b4) as having disjunctive predicates.

11. In the present interpretation, this concession is slightly understated: the full import of the sentence is better conveyed by the obviously parallel earlier remark at 96b15. The potential for confusion on this point is undoubtedly magnified by the close paronymous relation between χρή and χρήσιμος.

12. It is true that the general topic originally introduced at the outset of *Prior Analytics* 1.27 and pursued throughout Chapters 27 and 28, how to acquire syllogistic premises generally, is not obviously concerned with demonstrative premises. However, beginning in Chapter 30 Aristotle makes it clear that the scope of his discussion includes the issue of finding suitable premises for demonstration. Hence, at 46a4 he claims that the general procedure for collecting syllogistic premises set out in previous chapters is applicable to every "art" (τέχνη) and "study" (μάθημα), and just a few lines later (at a8) he cements the point by claiming that the recommended method is appropriate in settings where one is interested in establishing truth as opposed to mere plausibility, which according to *Topics* 1.1.100a27 is precisely what distinguishes demonstrative from dialectical reasoning.

13. There is no real question that the notion of explanatoriness operative in *Posterior Analytics* 1.2 is an objective one: the causativity condition (f) is metaphysical on its face, and although Aristotle does officially recognize wholly subjective senses of "better known than" and (epistemological) "priority," he is careful in the present context to exclude these at 71b31 by explicitly making the sort

of priority he has in mind a consequence of causativity (which, again, is plainly metaphysical). In fact, b34–72a5 disambiguate objective and subjective senses of γνωριμωτέρων respectively as that which is so "by nature" (τῇ φύσει) or "simpliciter" (ἁπλῶς), and that which is so "in relation to us" (πρὸς ἡμᾶς). And while Aristotle doesn't quite say there that demonstrative premises must be better known in the first sense, numerous passages noted in Barnes (1975) from *Topics* (6.4, passim), *Physics* (1.1, passim), *Metaphysics* (Z.3.1029b3–12), *Nicomachean Ethics* (1.4.1095b2–4) and *Prior Analytics* (2.23.68b35–37) make it virtually certain that his view is that a proper explanation explains what is better known to us (more familiar) in terms of what is better known simpliciter (more intelligible).

14. As against the view of Barnes discussed above in chapter 1, note 4.

15. These include, but are not limited to, the subject's essential attributes. See part 2 below.

16. See chapter 1, note 11 above.

17. *Sophist* 218B–E and 235A–C.

18. The full range of these immediate connections will be surveyed in part 2.

19. Again, as we shall see in part 2, Aristotle's full theory allows the range of the nonaccidental (and hence the scientifically interesting) to exceed by far what might be thought of quite narrowly as essential connections between terms.

20. *Posterior Analytics* 1.8.75b21–24.

21. The main burden of chapter 7 below will be to investigate the ramifications for Aristotle's theory of allowing the premises of demonstration to include statements expressing immediate negative connections at *Posterior Analytics* 1.15.79a33–b5.

22. It also follows that the possibility of finite demonstration (that is, one containing a finite number of syllogistic inferences) requires that there be at most a finite number of middle terms between the subject and predicate of the demonstrated statement. Aristotle undertakes to establish this possibility as a general theorem (for any statement whatever) in the so-called compactness proof of *Posterior Analytics* 1.19–23 (on which see also Lear [1980]).

23. There is some mystery about why Aristotle should be so confident of this uniqueness condition, given that he recognizes the existence of propria terms, which he defines in *Topics* 1.5 as convertible (that is to say, coextensive) with their subjects (102a18–19). The most likely solution is that in *Posterior Analytics* 2.13 he is restricting his attention to essence-signifying terms.

24. Compare chapter 1, note 22 above.

25. These representations are equivalent in the light of Aristotle's view in *Metaphysics* Z12 that the species within a genus are "equal to" (ἴσα; that is, one-to-one with) the differentiae that distinguish them.

26. If the independent assumption that divisions must be dichotomous is dropped, this will be the union of D's codifferentiae.

27. Here again we see implicit reliance by Aristotle on the compactness result of *Posterior Analytics* 1.19–23.

28. More detail on the nature and demonstrative function of such terms will be given in chapter 6.

29. Though my general view is that it is wrong to identify what Aristotle refers to as the (epistemological) "starting points" (ἀρχαί) of a demonstrative science with the ultimate premises of his syllogistic demonstrations, a comparison of this occurrence with 43b1 leaves little doubt that here he is thinking narrowly of *syllogistic* starting points (i.e., immediate premises).

30. The variation on this procedure given in this passage, and Aristotle's suggestion that there might be two kinds of proof for universal negatives, are inconsequential effects of the fact that propositions of this form are subject to contraposition of subject and predicate. In Aristotle's system, "No A is C" and "No C is A" are two distinct (albeit equivalent) propositions requiring distinct (albeit equivalent) syllogistic proofs.

31. Understanding "that whose existence is assumed" as a subject-genus is justified by the close parallel with 76b13–14.

32. Hintikka (1972), 63.

33. Ibid., 62.

34. Ibid.

35. Ibid. (emphasis mine).

36. See *Metaphysics* 7.17.1041a12–20.

37. In chapter 2 I shall argue that Aristotle's version of division, unlike Plato's, is also to be distinguished from the activity of conceptual analysis because he does not view it as a method for discovering definitions.

38. Given that the general method is meant to apply to the mathematical sciences, whose objects are not concrete, it is hardly likely that Aristotle would insist that the confrontation be perceptual. What is essential is that the divider have some epistemological grasp of his subjects.

39. It is possible that this point is grounded further in Aristotle's view that one cannot know "what something is" (τί ἐστι—that is, have an account of its essence—*Posterior Analytics* 2.10.93b29) without knowing "that it is" (εἰ ἔστι). See *Posterior Analytics* 1.1.71a26–29, 2.2.90a1–24, 2.8.93a14–29, 2.10.93b29–35.

40. In fact, there is some evidence, though it is hardly conclusive, that Aristotle's own classifications of animals in his *Historia Animalium* presuppose a system of types of animal-differentiae, such as means of locomotion, perception, and reproduction, which then guides the empirical study of the specific differentiae within these types that are exhibited by various kinds of animals.

41. Evidently, neither Plato nor Aristotle requires that these divisions be dichotomous. In fact, Cherniss (1944) suggests that a large part of Aristotle's dissatisfaction with Speusippus's brand of διαίρεσις stems from the fact that it permits only dichotomous divisions.

42. The problem of fitting the nonlogical common axioms, such as the alternation of proportionals (74a17–25), or the preservation of equality through sub-

traction and addition (76a40–b2), into a syllogistic model of proof is really one aspect of the general problem of how mathematical proof and syllogistic demonstration are related.

43. Perhaps the most obvious (and most embarrassing) difficulties for strict syllogisticism involve these "common axioms" (κοινὰ ἀξιώματα) such as the Laws of Noncontradiction and Excluded Middle, or the principle that equals taken from equals yield equals. The difficulty is that such principles (or restricted versions of them) are unambiguously placed among the ἀρχαί of demonstration by passages in group B (*Posterior Analytics* 1.10.76a41–42; 77a10–35), and yet as a matter of simple syntax they manifestly do not match any of the four general propositional forms out of which the *Prior Analytics* insists all (nonmodal) syllogisms must be constructed (*Prior Analytics* 1.1.24a17–20). Indeed, it appears that neither Ross (1949) nor Hintikka (1972) is ready to saddle Aristotle with the highly dubious contention that the common axioms are ultimate syllogistic premises. According to Ross, they are "not premises but the principles according to which we reason" (56), and according to Hintikka they are "those and only those assumptions on which the whole structure of Aristotelian syllogisms is based" (59). This is why I said earlier that there probably are no actual cases of pure strict syllogisticism.

44. The details of this peculiar little argument will be taken up in chapter 5.

CHAPTER 2: DEMONSTRATION AND DEFINITION

1. Compare also *Prior Analytics* 2.21.67a5–27.
2. Solmsen (1929). But cf. Ross (1949) and chapter 1 above.
3. *Posterior Analytics* 76a32–37; b1–23; 93b29–33.
4. See especially *Topics* 6, passim. Aristotle is quite aware that since a paradigmatic definition involves reference to the defined species, the genus, and the differentia, it gives the appearance of containing three rather than two terms, and hence of not being simple enough to instantiate the elementary form of the universal affirmative proposition of *Prior Analytics* 1.1.2. That this is merely an appearance is the very substance of the "unity of definition" thesis at *De Interpretatione* 5.17a9–15, *Posterior Analytics* 2.6.92a30–34, and *Metaphysics* 7.12.1037b8–38.
5. I am not persuaded by Hintikka's (1972) attempt to discount this and a parallel passage (*Posterior Analytics* 1.2.72a20–21) by claiming that both employ εἶναι in its "predicative" rather than its "existential" role (67). His reasons for this are not obvious, but they may be based on the quasi-linguistic analysis of εἶναι and its cognates found in Kahn (1973). According to that analysis, there is no "independent" use of εἶναι in early Greek, and all sentences of the form "X is" should be understood as equivalent to predicative statements of the form "X is something or other," where this latter means that there is at least one property had by X (page 15, note 8). The problem I find with this analysis is that it seems

to confuse the obvious truth that for anything to exist it must have at least one property with the controversial proposal that the statement that X exists is logically equivalent to (perhaps even synonymous with) the statement that X has at least one property. This same objection is developed independently in Roberts (1982).

6. The inference may not be immediate. Jacobs (1979) contains a plausible argument that the existential import of genuine premises is thought by Aristotle to follow from a more fundamental requirement that they always either affirm "something of something" (τι κατά τινος) or deny "something to something" (τι ἀπό τινος), where the use of the indefinite pronouns imports presuppositions of existence.

7. Compare *Posterior Analytics* 2.3–10.

8. Hintikka (1972) correctly observes that the term ἄμεσος is sometimes also used to denote these statements of immediate connection between terms, but that in its normal usage (as for instance, at *Posterior Analytics* 1.2.72a8) it picks out propositions that are "immediate" in the sense that they are underived.

9. Barnes (1975), 94–95.

10. Moreover, for reasons to be discussed shortly, this problem cannot be overcome by simply adding a statement of general existence to Barnes's analysis, so that it reads, If anything is a pair, then *a* knows that it is even, and there are pairs.

11. These will certainly include all past and present men, though there may be some question about whether Aristotle's puzzle in *De Interpretatione* 9 regarding singular statements about the future rules out the possibility that (2) could also involve reference to all future men.

12. Notice that this is not to say that under this interpretation sentence (2) is *synonymous* with a conjunction of singular *sentences*. In fact, another way to characterize the transparency feature discussed above is to say that one could on this interpretation know that all of the singular propositions expressed by (2) were true without having any idea of which propositions those were.

13. Even singular statements like "a is F" are thought to introduce existential import only insofar as they entail statements of general existence (by Existential Generalization). Incidentally, I can find no evidence whatever that Aristotle has any such theoretical notion of general existence, though he of course uses sentences that *we* might analyze as expressing it. For this reason (among others) I cannot agree with the proposal in Hintikka (1972) to interpret the existence assumptions of Aristotelian science (e.g. at *Posterior Analytics* 76a32–7, 76b1–23, 93b29–33) as expressible by statements of the form "There are Fs" (62–63). In chapter 5 I shall argue that Aristotle even regards the existential import of particular statements, such as "Some numbers are even," as singular in nature and as stemming likewise from the referential function of their grammatical subjects.

14. On this distinction see Kneale (1936) and Moore (1936).

15. This of course is not to deny that the truth-values of the sentences are perfectly correlated. Both sentences will be true in all (and only) those worlds where

there are men (i.e., some referents of "Every man"), and all of those are also animals.

16. This may be equivalent, though it certainly would not be recognizable to Aristotle as such, to a Fregean-style statement expressing a certain constraint on the possibilities of predicate-satisfaction (or kind-membership) among all (actual or possible) individuals within some domain of discourse: If anything is a man, then (necessarily) it is an animal.

17. Tredennick (1938) translates ἕξις here as "faculty," which is normally reserved for the Greek δύναμις. However, in view of the fact that Aristotle goes on at 99b26–34 to *argue* that this preexistent condition must be some sort of δύναμις, (that is, an epistemic proclivity, as opposed to an occurrent cognitive state), it is better to understand him as deliberately employing the wider term ἕξις at b18 in a sense that includes, but is not limited to, δυνάμεις.

18. On this see Kahn (1981).

19. It is plausible that this use of λανθάνω is meant to pick up Plato's use of ἀναμιμνήσκω at *Meno* 85E and 86B.

20. The deployment of the potentiality versus actuality distinction to steer between the horns of an apparent dilemma is of course vintage Aristotle (cf., for example, his definition of κίνησις in *Physics* 3.1, and his treatments of growth and perception in *De Anima* 2.4 and 5 respectively), which raises the question of whether its occurrence in this early work might be a later intrusion. This hypothesis is weakened by the fact that the term ἐντελέχεια, with which δύναμις is regularly contrasted in later works, does not occur at all in this chapter.

21. This would have the unfortunate consequence that in some sense any animal, qua sentient, has the capacity to apprehend such principles.

22. Compare 100a14–b17. The interdependence between Aristotle's metaphysics and epistemology on this point will be discussed shortly.

23. The role of intuition in ἐπαγωγή is discussed in detail in Kahn (1981), Kosman (1973), and Lesher (1973).

24. For an interesting and comprehensive study of this more elevated conception of αἴσθησις, see Modrak (1987).

25. Notice that this intensional interpretation of the results of Platonic Division is not affected by the fact that the *evidence* the method employs seems to be constituted by more or less empirical observations that certain classes of individuals are subdivided into "natural" subkinds (but at the same time, my use of the adjective *natural* here certainly bears much metaphysical weight).

26. Aristotle's immanent realism and its effect on his epistemology will be discussed at length later in this chapter.

27. Burnyeat (1970), Fine (1979), and Nehamas (1983).

28. There is a close Aristotelian parallel to this Platonic notion of an interrelational logos in *Metaphysics* Z12, where it is asserted that an adequate definition, by containing the final differentia of the definiendum, can be thought to make implicit reference to all the differentiae of which that is a specification. Of course,

Aristotle never says that such a logos itself conveys knowledge of the highest sort.

29. Burnyeat (1981).

30. See chapter 1.

31. See chapter 2, note 5 above.

32. *Posterior Analytics* 2.3.90b33.

33. Actually, this question is first raised and treated dialectically in Chapter 3 at 90b28–91a12, but Aristotle does not begin to develop his own answer to it until the beginning of Chapter 4.

34. Owen (1961).

35. The argument is actually a bit more complicated than I have represented it. Aristotle argues that an "immediate" statement can sometimes occur as a syllogistic conclusion, but only if both premises of the syllogism are biconditional, or, as he puts it, they can both be converted (ἀντιστρέφειν), in which case there is a *petitio principii,* and hence no genuine demonstration (91a25–b10).

36. The attenuation requires a play on the terms δείκνυμι ("to show or display") and ἀποδείκνυμι ("to demonstrate or prove"), so that a "definition" can be said to be "demonstrated" in the sense that the τι ἐστι it expresses is "revealed" or "displayed" by the arrangement of the premises of a demonstrative syllogism.

37. This view, which originated in Lukasiewicz (1957), is propounded in Mansion (1976), moderated somewhat in Mansion (1981), and criticized in Chapter 12 of Sorabji (1980).

38. Of course, the restriction to substantial, or natural, kinds here is crucial, since Aristotle certainly does not think one could gain scientific knowledge of an individual by studying necessary relations among its nonessential properties (*Posterior Analytics* 1.6.75a18–27). This is not to say that he believes knowledge of systematic relations among accidents (i.e., nonsubstances) is impossible (on which, see his discussion of the possibility of sciences of nonsubstantial accidents in *Metaphysics* Γ4), but only that the objects of such knowledge would not be the subjects of those accidents.

39. Unfortunately, the significance of this is obscured even from Aristotle himself in the *Organon* by the fact that he regularly collapses these two very different types of metaphysical connection into a single relation (the said-of relation in the *Categories,* or type 1 per se belonging in *Posterior Analytics*). On the other hand, the *Metaphysics* distinguishes sharply between the two relations and focuses especially on the relation between individual and proximate kind.

CHAPTER 3: THE CHARACTER OF DEMONSTRATIVE PREMISES

1. I mean here to contrast general epistemology (that is, the philosophical analysis of the general concepts of knowledge, belief, justification, and so on) such as what occurs in the *Theaetetus,* with special investigations into the nature of specific forms of knowledge and justification. Examples of special epistemol-

ogy are quite common in Aristotle's works. For instance, the *Topics* is an investigation of *dialectical* knowledge, the *Nicomachean Ethics* analyzes the nature of *practical* knowledge, and (as suggested in my introduction) the *Posterior Analytics* presents a theory of *demonstrative* (or scientific) knowledge.

2. White (1972), 60, Patzig (1969).

3. I argue in Ferejohn (1976) that Aristotle's curious views about the validity of mixed modal syllogisms in the *Prior Analytics* (e.g., at 30a21–24 and 30b7–10) cannot be explained satisfactorily by the suggestion that he is insensitive to subtle differences in the scope of modal operators. The fact is that there are other places (e.g., *De Interpretatione* 9.19a29–33) where he shows himself to be quite sensitive to such matters. Moreover, I argue there is a high degree of systematicity in Aristotle's results, which is not accounted for by the hypothesis that they rest on confusion.

4. Hintikka (1957).

5. This last inference presents some problems in interpretation. On its face, the Aristotelian sentence at 73a24, since it contains a plural form, ἐξ ἀναγκαίων, to denote the premis*es* of a demonstration, seems to assert that the necessity of the conclusion of a demonstration requires the necessity of both premises. However, Alexander of Aphrodisias tells us that the modal principle that requires this (namely, the so-called *peiorem* rule that the conclusion of a modal syllogism can be no stronger than its weakest premise) was developed by Aristotle's successor, Theophrastus. Moreover, it is violated by Aristotle himself at *Prior Analytics* 30a15. Hence, either Aristotle has chosen an unfortunate way of expressing a result that is consistent with his logical theory (namely that the necessity of the conclusion requires the necessity of at least one premise), or he is here importing some extralogical (perhaps epistemological) reason that both premises of a *demonstrative* syllogism must be necessary. Evidence for the latter hypothesis is to be found at *Posterior Analytics* 74b13ff.

6. Even though Aristotle's discussion in *Posterior Analytics* 1.4–10 appears to restrict the immediate premises of demonstration only to affirmative statements, he makes it quite clear in Chapter 15 that his full theory also allows negative premises expressing immediate exclusion relations (79a33–36). The place of such negative predications in the theory of demonstration will be the principal topic of chapter 7.

7. In fact, Aristotle attaches these subconditions to the attributes ascribed by such sentences. I represent them as conditions on the relation between subject and predicate for convenience of exposition, since his remarks are always meant to apply to an attribute *as applied to a certain subject*.

8. *Topics* 103b8, 109a10, 125a6, 149b12, 163a32.

9. It has been suggested by some writers, e.g. Code (1986) and Lennox (1987), that since as a general rule, the expression "*qua*" (ᾗ) is used by Aristotle as an intensional idiom, the "qua itself" condition on catholic predications therefore pertains to an intensional relation between subject and predicate, perhaps that

the predicate applies to a certain class of things when they are conceived of or described as falling under the subject term. On such a view, Aristotle might allow that there could be two sciences that study exactly the same genus of things but are nonetheless distinct sciences because one studies them qua Fs and the other studies them qua Gs. I certainly do not deny there are many occurrences of ᾗ in Aristotle that do carry this intensional meaning (as, for instance, in his "definition" of κίνησις at *Physics* 3.1); and there are clear precedents for this use in Plato (e.g., in *Republic* 1 and 4). What I do deny is that the expression is always used this way, and that it is so used in *Posterior Analytics* 1.4 in particular. For the intensional reading is at odds with the fact that the test Aristotle proposes for the condition is given there in extensional terms: he speaks of the "*first* subject" (going downward) to possess the attribute, or the "last differentia" (going upward), whose removal also removes the attribute, and these ordinals are evidently connected to some sequence of inclusion relations. A key passage on this issue is 74a38–b4. There Aristotle contorts himself so far as to make *bronze* a peculiar sort of differentia of isosceles triangle just so that he can extend the inclusion-sequence, *plane figure → triangle → isosceles triangle*, one more step to *bronze isosceles triangle* in order to apply this extensional test. (Hence, I think this passage should be contrasted with *Metaphysics* Z.8.1033a24–b5, where virtually the same example is employed, but the *qua* must be taken intensionally.)

10. It is remarkable that despite the relative clarity of these pronouncements, there are some who would still deny that Aristotle is committed to the view that all per se predications are necessary. I am referring here to views expressed in White (1972) and Hintikka (1957).

11. The passage also introduces a use of the expression "*per accidens*" (κατὰ συμβεβηκός) corresponding to each of the four uses of *per se* presented and discussed. These uses, which Aristotle says at 73b4,5 and 11,12 are strictly complementary to the corresponding uses of *per se,* can be ignored until chapter 6.

CHAPTER 4: TYPE 1 PER SE PREDICATION

1. This should not be confused with the historical thesis that the *Categories* represents a relatively immature stage of Aristotle's thought, whereas the *Analytics* were written during a later stage of his development. My claim is simply that, for whatever reason, the *Analytics* present a more complicated and sophisticated semantical system than what is found in the *Categories*. I take this to be compatible both with the "juvenalia" view of the *Categories* just described, and with what may be called the "primer" view of that work, according to which it is seen as a sort of propaedeutic, written in full awareness of Aristotle's more subtle views, which he intended to introduce new students to philosophy. As these remarks suggest, I am assuming here that at least the first five chapters of the *Categories* are Aristotle's own work, though my contentions here would not be materially affected if it should turn out that it is an "Aristotelian" treatise by another hand.

2. This translation is from Ackrill (1963).

3. Moravcsik (1967).

4. Ackrill (1963), 71.

5. Ackrill (1963), 78.

6. It might be argued against this interpretation of *Categories* 4 that Aristotle's characterization of affirmations (and denials) at 2a2–8 as "what are true or false" is merely meant to distinguish them from terms, which are described right afterward (at a8–9) as not incapable of bearing truth-values. On this view, the remark is seen as closely parallel to *De Interpretatione* 1.16a14–19, a passage where Aristotle is concerned simply to introduce the central subject of the work (statements) by distinguishing them from various other kinds of linguistic entities. The problem I find with this alternative is that it does not attach any importance to, or give any explanation of, the fact that the *Categories* chapter (unlike *De Interpretatione* 1) explicitly states both that the possibility of truth or falsity is generated by the interweaving of uncombined expressions, and (immediately beforehand, at b25–a4) that each of these uncombined expressions signifies an entity in one or another of the categories. The proximity of these points creates the presumption that they are intended to be closely connected, and on my view they are: the semantic values (truth and falsity) of combined expressions (statements) are partly determined by the semantic values (significata) of the uncombined expressions (terms) that comprise them. Incidentally, this interpretation of *Categories* 4 makes the chapter an Aristotelian echo of *Sophist* 261D–263B, where Plato says not only that truth and falsity apply exclusively to complex expressions (statements) produced by the interweaving of at least one verb ($\acute{\rho}\hat{\eta}\mu\alpha$) and one noun ($\check{o}\nu o\mu\alpha$), but also that this is because a verb signifies an action, a noun signifies a subject of action, and a true (or false) statement is one whose verb signifies an action that is in fact performed (or not) by what its noun signifies.

7. That this semantics is limited to what I have called atomic sentences is evidenced by the choice of examples at 1a18: "Man runs" ($\check{\alpha}\nu\theta\rho\omega\pi o\varsigma$ $\tau\rho\acute{\epsilon}\chi\epsilon\iota$) and "Man wins" ($\check{\alpha}\nu\theta\rho\omega\pi o\varsigma$ $\nu\iota\kappa\hat{\alpha}$). At 2a6–7 he indicates that "denials" ($\grave{\alpha}\pi\acute{o}\phi\alpha\sigma\epsilon\iota\varsigma$) as well as "affirmations" ($\kappa\alpha\tau\acute{\alpha}\phi\alpha\sigma\epsilon\iota\varsigma$) could be formed by combination, but he is apparently not concerned in *Categories* to analyze sentences involving negation. However, in *De Interpretatione,* Chapters 10 and 11, he can be seen extending this rudimentary semantics to sentences involving negation, as well as to general sentences containing "all" or "some."

8. Furth (1988), 9–15.

9. Ibid., 12.

10. It's not actually clear whether this is exactly the way the analysis is supposed to go, or whether instead the first step is really part of the analysis and not just a regimentation that precedes it. On this alternative view, the "deep structure" expressed by Socrates is F" is that Fness is *predicated of* Socrates, where *predicated-of* is a generic ontological relation that has *said-of* and *inherence* as exhaustive subrelations. Obviously, as a practical matter it is extremely difficult

to separate these two alternative views, since Aristotle observes no clear distinction between object language and metalanguage.

11. Ackrill (1963).

12. See Owen (1965a).

13. Especially 2a11–14, 2a27–b6, and 3a7–21.

14. Here again we see Aristotle conflating class membership and class inclusion; they appear in the *Categories* as undifferentiated subtypes of the said-of relation. On this, see Frede (1978).

15. Obviously, the overall intelligibility of the tetrachotomy depends in large part on the proposition that there is a real distinction between Aristotelian substances (entities of type [i] and [ii]) and the types of entities that fall into the third and fourth divisions. While this might seem so obvious from a modern point of view that we would be inclined to excuse a writer for simply assuming its truth and intelligibility, the problem of making out the exact nature of this distinction between substance and nonsubstance was apparently both crucial and difficult for Aristotle, for he expends considerable effort working on it in *Categories* 5, and returns to it with a vengeance later in the middle books of the *Metaphysics*. This preoccupation has led many writers to the opinion that understanding Aristotle's views on this matter is an important key to understanding his metaphysics. Furth (1988), for one, seems to be of this opinion, and accordingly he devotes considerable space to supporting and developing the suggestion that the distinction in question ultimately rests in the *Categories* on Aristotle's observation that substance-terms are *individuative*, more or less as that term is explicated by Quine (1960), while nonsubstance terms are not. This is an extremely important matter that must eventually be sorted out, but it falls outside the scope of the present work. I shall return to it briefly below in order to suggest that Aristotle's emphasis on the substance versus nonsubstance distinction is evidently reinforced by the methodology he employs in the *Categories* to arrive at his list of categories.

16. Furth (1988), who is inclined toward the view that the *Categories* was written in full view of the doctrines of the *Metaphysics,* and consequently that such matters are already on Aristotle's mind in the *Categories,* composes a fictional "essentializing addendum" to Chapter 5 of the *Categories* that takes up the distinction between substance and nonsubstance. While I admit that such questions follow naturally from Aristotle's discussion in Chapter 5, I can find no evidence that Aristotle himself is aware of them in the *Categories*.

17. In fact, he says so little about type (iii) (non-substantial particulars) that there has been a considerable amount of disagreement among some of the best modern Aristotelian scholars about whether they should be taken as *maximally specific universals* (that is, things necessarily capable of being shared by more than one subject; cf. Owen [1965a] and Frede [1978]), or whether they are instead some sort of abstract individuals (things that necessarily can inhere only in a single subject; cf. Ackrill [1963]).

18. And perhaps also type (iii) entities, if the "maximally specific universal" view of them discussed in the preceding note is correct.

19. In particular, there appears no way of telling from what he says in the *Organon* whether he thinks of the higher kinds within his categorial network in a purely *extensional* way (as classes of primary substances or nonsubstantial particulars), or whether he thinks of them rather as some sort of *intensions* (what modern philosophical logicians call "properties"), or whether he thinks of them in some other way altogether different from both of these.

20. Compare Furth (1988), 14.

21. Compare Owen (1965b) for an intriguing explanation of how the "bifurcated" semantics of the *Categories* represents at least one Aristotelian attempt to construct a theory of predication immune from defects charged against Platonic predication in the "Third Man argument."

22. Aristotle did not give up entirely on the project of giving some further explication of inherence relations. I shall argue in chapter Six that the type 4 per se predications discussed at *Posterior Analytics* 1.4.73b10–16, which would have to be classified as expressing the inherence relation in the *Categories,* are not thought by Aristotle to be fortuitous.

23. Ackrill (1963), 79–80.

24. Compare Grene (1963), 58.

25. Notice that this single question is also the first in the list of most basic questions posed in the multiple-question method. I shall argue presently that its presence in both methods has an impact on Aristotle's choice of terminology in *Posterior Analytics* 1.4.

26. As in my account of the multiple-question method, I am here presenting an English version of the procedure. As before, in Greek a correct answer could very naturally take the form of a one- or two-word sentence fragment.

27. The details of this "compactness" proof are reconstructed in chapter 2 of Lear (1980).

28. This assortment illustrates once more that the requirements for membership in the initial collection of the single-question method are indeed quite liberal. It is not even limited to particulars, as is shown by the inclusion of items (iii) and (vi). In fact each of the divisions in the tetrachotomy of *Categories* 2 is represented here.

29. I am not claiming that these are the very chains Aristotle would have generated if he had performed step 2 of the single-question method on items (i)–(vi), or even that they are very close. These examples are offered merely to show the formal operation of the method, and not to reflect any substantive Aristotelian assumptions about natural kinds.

30. On the other hand, these assumptions entail nothing about the number of such hierarchies required to categorize "everything there is" (πάντα τὰ ὄντα), and this may be why Aristotle evidently feels free to experiment with his list of categories.

31. Ackrill (1963), 80.

32. Ibid.

33. Ackrill's account, while appealing, does not explain why this alleged shift

in Aristotle's ways of thinking of the categories should be so sudden as to occur within a mere five lines of text. Apparently recognizing this difficulty, Ackrill closes his brief discussion of *Topics* 1.9 in the modest tones of a recommendation that the chapter is in need of further study.

Incidentally, it may be not only Aristotle's terminological choices but also his substantive views that are affected by his vacillating attitude toward the construction of the categories. In particular, the tetrachotomy of *Categories* 2, which we saw above to depend crucially on the intelligibility of the substance versus non-substance distinction, is a doctrine that could very likely occur to one thinking in terms of the multiple-question method, since that method presupposes the ability to pick out substance from nonsubstances. On the other hand, it would not be so obvious if one has in mind the single-question method, to which the substance versus non-substance distinction is not essential.

34. More precisely, the suggestion is that relation E includes, but extends beyond, the earlier relation. My reason for resisting a simple identification of the two relations is based on the presence in the *Posterior Analytics* of what might be termed "constructive" definitions, such as "Triangle =df a plane figure enclosed by three straight lines," which were apparently in vogue among the proto-Euclidean geometries with which Aristotle was probably conversant. Aristotle may be alluding to something like this at 73a35–38 when he says that *line* is in the what-is-it of *triangle,* for there is no reason to think that he would be committed in the *Categories* to holding that *line* is said of *triangle.* I thank Mohan Matthen for first pointing out to me the incongruence between Aristotle's examples of type 1 *per se* predication at *Posterior Analytics* 1.4, and a strict genus and differentia conception of definition.

CHAPTER 5: TYPE 2 PER SE PREDICATION

1. This translation is from Ackrill (1963). In an earlier work, Ferejohn (1981), I took the presence of both λέγεται and κατηγορεῖται in this passage to indicate that Aristotle is announcing a more complicated principle, which I labeled "vicarious predication," involving both the said-of relation and the generic predication relation. I thank Montgomery Furth and Michael Frede for convincing me this is just an illusion created by the fact that Aristotle often uses the two verbs interchangeably.

2. See chapter 5, note 6 below.

3. Notice that on the suggestion in chapter 4 that relation E of the *Posterior Analytics* is the descendant of the said-of relation in the *Categories,* it becomes very easy to see why Aristotle assigns the properties of *transitivity* and *participation* to the ancestor relation. For it should be immediately obvious that the relation that orders terms into the hierarchical structures generated by the single-question method described in chapter 4 is transitive. And if it is understood that a definition is a λόγος signifying the what-is-it, it follows directly from transitivity

that the definition of any predicate that belongs in the what-is-it of given subject will itself belong—in fact, belong per se—to that subject. This last is not to imply that the other sort of type 1 per se predications (those that correspond to the constructive definitions mentioned in chapter 4, note 34) satisfy either of these conditions.

4. On this, see chapter 1 above.

5. *Prior Analytics* 21a26, 49b5, *Topics* 101b39–102a1, 130a39, 142b2–6, 147b13–15, 149a1–2, b3–5.

6. This is followed immediately (at 1a28–34) by the observation that there are some special cases, e.g., that of whiteness (τὸ λευκόν), where the name of the inherent is applicable to what it inheres in, but that even in those cases the logos fails to apply. As Furth (1988) has pointed out (19), this records Aristotle's appreciation of the linguistic happenstance that the adjectival form λευκόν performed extra duty in Greek by occasionally standing in for the noun form λευκότης as the *name* of whiteness.

7. If this is correct, and Aristotle can be interpreted as doing better on this issue in, say, the *Metaphysics,* that should count as some evidence, though it is certainly not conclusive, for the view that the *Categories* is an earlier work. Cf. chapter 4, note 1 above. Against this, Frede (1978) maintains that Aristotle's "later" treatment of differentiae in the *Metaphysics* is already in view in the *Categories.*

8. Ackrill (1963), 85–87.

9. *Metaphysics* 7.12. 1037b8–1038a35.

10. Dancy (1975) and Kung (1977).

11. This is reinforced by the usual placement of the *Topics* as earlier than *Categories,* for that would make it very easy to understand how Aristotle could here innocently make use of the term in ignorance of its later philosophical significance.

12. This contrasts with *Metaphysics* Z.12, where Aristotle is open to the possibility that differentiae can be classified by the differentiae kinds to which they belong. For instance, at 1038a14–15 he suggests that *"cloven-footedness"* (ἡ σχιζοποδία) is "a certain (subtype of) *footedness"* (ποδότης τις), which suggests that one could construct hierarchical classifications of differentiae as well as the kinds they divide. I thank Allan Gotthelf for this point.

13. This second definitional relation takes on an even greater importance in later works. For in addition to its application to the case of differentia and genus (which emerge out of the late Platonic conception of definition), Aristotle eventually comes in *Metaphysics* Z.5 (1030b17–22) to believe that essentially the same definitional relation holds between what he calls the "per se affection" (καθ᾽αὑτά πάθος) *snubness,* and its proper material subject (*nose*), and in *Metaphysics* Z.10 and 11 he goes on to exploit what he sees as important affinities between this homely example and the crucial philosophical issue of characterizing the relation between a composite substance (e.g., a particular man) and its appropriate (proximate) material (blood, flesh, bone, etc.). The details of this latter procedure are taken up in Ferejohn (unpublished).

14. This, incidentally, is the view shared by Aristotle's ancient commentators: see I. Philoponus, *In Analytica Posteriora*, f.16 (Brandis 204a48–b3), and Themistius, *In Analytica Posteriora*, f.3 (Brandis 204a39–40).

15. It is admittedly peculiar to find Aristotle using the nominal expression τὰ ἀντικείμενα in an adverbial sense without the addition of a preposition. But however strange this may seem, the occurrence of this expression opposite the familiar ἁπλῶς in an ἤ . . . ἤ . . . construction leaves little doubt that he is doing just that. The text may suffer from some defect in the manuscript tradition (perhaps the omission of a κατά), but if so the defect is now hidden, since none of the important manuscripts vary from this reading.

16. This view is corroborated by Philoponus, f.16b (Brandis 204b13–18).

17. The notion of absolute necessity here is apparently unconnected with that discussed in chapter 2 of Patzig (1969).

18. But cf. the "essentializing addendum to *Categories* 5" in Furth (1988) and chapter 4, note 16 above on that subject.

19. The central argument of chapter 7 below is that both writers perceive and react to what they see as serious conceptual difficulties with the employment of negative predicates in insufficiently restricted contexts, as would be required, for instance, to state that everything whatever (including living things) is either odd or not odd.

20. These will of course include differentiae, but may not be limited to them. Aristotle does not seem sure about what to do with pairs such as (male, female), on which see *Metaphysics* 10.9.1058a29–b26.

21. It might be objected here that on this interpretation the argument doesn't really establish the necessity of opposites, since STRONG MLEM itself implies that any opposite is possessed necessarily by its subjects. While this objection has force, it should not be thought to convict Aristotle (on this interpretation) of outright circularity. Rather, the argument should be understood as making epistemological headway by showing how the necessity implicit in what might be termed the "essentialistic bifurcation" of a division by opposites distributes to the connections between those attributes taken separately and their respective subjects. Hence, the argument should not be viewed as a demonstration of the necessity of type 2 per se predications on the basis of their nonmodal properties, but rather as proceeding from the assumption that a certain genus contains a necessary partition to the conclusion that each of its members necessarily possesses one or the other of the pair of opposites that jointly effect that partition.

22. Barnes (1975), 115.

23. Barnes doesn't actually distinguish the stronger and weaker interpretations of MLEM, but he presumably prefers the weaker.

24. Barnes (1975), 115. Aristotle's aim in the *Prior Analytics* 1.31 passages cited (46b3–19, 30–35) is essentially polemical and anti-Platonic. His point, which is reiterated at *Posterior Analytics* 2.5.91b35–92a5, is that the proponent of the method of division errs in supposing that he can move by logical means

directly from, say, (i) All men are either mortal or immortal, to (ii) All men are mortal. The mistake here, according to Aristotle, lies in the fact that the choice of mortality over immortality (or neither) as a distinguishing feature of men is left unsupported, so that this reasoning simply assumes the truth of (ii) and therefore begs the question (46b12, 18, 33), whereas (ii) can and should be proved by syllogistic means (46a36–39). What Aristotle does *not* say, and what Barnes tries to read into these passages, is that these means will necessarily incorporate the use of (i) or some other disjunctive predication as a syllogistic premise. Similarly, the schematic arguments in *Prior Analytics* 1.46 and 2.22 to which Barnes points (51b39–41, 52a34–37, 68a3–16) are certainly not presented in explicit syllogistic form and seem to be among the inference patterns that Aristotle regards as genuinely deductive but not syllogistic in character (Cf. 47a23–25).

25. Compare Bonitz (1870), 9b53–55. One interesting secondary result of the extremely compelling argument in Frede (1978) in support of Owen's "maximally specific" interpretation of nonsubstantial particulars (cf. Owen [1965a] and chapter 4, note 17 above) is that even the indefinite sentences of the *Categories*, where Aristotle is not concerned with the general sentence forms of the syllogistic, should be interpreted as particular statements. In particular, Frede's main argument relies partly on the correct observation that the indefinite sentence, "White inheres in body," at *Categories* 5.2a31–32 must be understood as asserting that some bodies are white.

26. This mistake is discussed in chapter 2 in connection with the interpretation of what I call "referential universals."

27. Of course, this need not be a proper subset, since where "Every S is P" is true, the singular propositions that make its consequence, "Some S is P" true are the very ones that underlie the truth of the universal statement itself. This is the reason one cannot move from "Some S is P" to "Some S is not P" in Aristotelian logic.

Geach (1962) attempts to undermine the intelligibility of this mode of interpretation by asking how it would treat a *false* statement of the form "Some S is P," and rejecting out of hand the response that it would then not be about any S at all. The reason behind this rejection is presumably the Russellian idea (pressed against Frege in "On Denoting") that determining the referents of the terms in a sentence should properly be prior to, and certainly not dependent upon, a determination of the sentence's truth-value. If so, it is curious that Geach should rely on this consideration, given that he himself takes pains to point out that the sort of "reference" involved is not *intended* (or speaker) reference, but a much "thinner," wholly semantic relation (7, 8). According to Geach, indeed, it is an entirely nonpsychological notion according to which the referents of the subject of a sentence are just those things the facts about which make the sentence true. Only by slipping back into thinking about intended reference does one find it problematic that reference should be posterior to truth-value.

28. It is important here to record a point that precisely matches one made in the earlier discussion of the referential universal in chapter 2, namely that the

transparency of the referential particular versions of (7b) and (8b) does not entail that they are each synonymous with conjunctions of singular statements (about the odd and even numbers respectively). To recall that earlier discussion (especially chapter 2, note 12), it would be entirely possible to know that a referential particular was true without knowing exactly which singular propositions made it true, even though the replacement of any of those propositions with different ones would result in the sentence being about a different group of individuals. So, for example, various covert departmental comings and goings could alter the reference of my utterance of "Some of my colleagues are in," through different occasions, and these alterations would change the content of my knowledge of its truth, even though its truth-value would remain unchanged so long as the department was not empty. I think it is failure to recognize this possibility that ultimately leads Geach to deny the intelligibility of referential particulars.

29. Since the reasoning at 73b22–24 involves equating the properties signified by *not odd* and *even,* it also is concerned with the necessity of such sentences as (7c) Some numbers are not odd, and (8c) Some numbers are not even. How exactly such predications figure in Aristotle's theory of demonstration is the main topic of chapter 7.

CHAPTER 6: TYPE 3 PER ACCIDENS AND TYPE 4 PER SE PREDICATION

1. This translation will be observed not to make obvious sense as it stands, since the referent of its subject is obscure. The usual and accepted manner of rectifying this, employed by both Mure (1928) and Tredennick (1938), is to supply a grammatical subject in English by inserting the catch-all noun *thing* after the adjective *white,* so that the translation reads (1′) The white *thing* is a man. In view of Aristotle's subsequent remarks at 81b27, it does appear that this device produces an English translation that comes close in meaning to the original Greek sentence. But at the same time, it does so by obscuring the reason Aristotle finds sentences like (1) interesting. For sentence (1′), unlike (1), is not an intercategorial predication with a nonsubstantial subject. Its supplied grammatical subject, "thing," is a very general sortal noun that comes close in meaning to Aristotle's own "substance" (οὐσία). Hence, (1′) would be classified as homocategorial by Aristotle, and therefore not of the type that interests him at 81b24–27. For this reason, I prefer the somewhat awkward translation of (1) given here, which at least has the virtue of reflecting the relevant categorial features of the original Greek. For it is quite usual in Greek to form a complete grammatical subject simply by prefacing a neuter adjectival form with an appropriate definite article, and there is no need to supply a grammatical subject by the use of placeholding nouns or pronouns. Hence, for Aristotle the only signifying expression that occurs in the subject part of (1) is the adjective *white.* And since this expression signifies a nonsubstance, this sentence is indeed an intercategorial predication with a nonsubstantial subject.

2. We are of course not talking about perfect context-independence, which would be tantamount to some sort of natural signification theory.

3. Incidentally, the absence of context-dependent semantical relations in Aristotle's *Organon* also explains why he is sometimes tempted to add to his ontology what are referred to in Matthews (1982) as "kooky objects," such as "cultured Mikkalos," who is said at *Prior Analytics* 47b30–338 to perish when Mikkalos becomes uncultured. For if Aristotle had no way to say that the expression "cultured Mikkalos" temporarily *refers* to Mikkalos, it is easy to see why he might be inclined to invent this peculiar temporary entity as the significatum of the combined expression.

4. Per accidens, that is, in all three of the other senses explicated in *Posterior Analytics* 1.4. In terms of the *Categories* semantics discussed in chapter 4, A and B must both inhere in S.

5. This sudden change of subject might not be out of the ordinary if Aristotle were engaged at 73a35–b16 in reporting the actual usages of the expressions *per se* and *per accidens* current among his contemporaries. However, all the available evidence indicates that he is contriving, and not just reporting, these uses.

6. Compare *Physics* 2.1 and chapter 3 above.

7. The point of these passages should not be overrated. There is no evidence for the claim that the *Categories* regards all true inherence-predications as fortuitous (and so as outside the domain of science). What we learn from the *De Interpretatione* 9 passage is that Aristotle recognizes some clear-cut instances of inherence-predications as fortuitous, and that he provides no means in the *Categories* to distinguish these from others that are not (if there are any such).

8. See my discussion in chapter 2 of the place of definitions in demonstration.

9. Especially in Book 1. On this see Barnes (1969).

10. Bonitz (1870), 177a53–54.

11. Cohen (1971).

12. Mure (1928).

13. Here it is important to distinguish sharply between generality and universality. Characterizing the subjects of ἐπὶ τὸ πολύ predications as general (as opposed to restricted) is not the same as saying that they are universal (as opposed to singular) in form. The first characterization is semantic and the second syntactic: one of the most general subject expressions I can imagine, "the thing," is syntactically a singular expression, whereas there are many universal expressions, e.g., "all black NFL coaches," that are not very general at all.

14. This curious temporal manner of characterizing necessary general truths has led Hintikka in a series of articles (collected and revised in Hintikka [1973]) to argue that Aristotle equates necessity and omnitemporality. This device can be explained alternatively, and more plausibly, if it is understood as a consequence of an understandable restriction of attention on the part of a natural scientist to sentences that describe correlations between repeatable event-types. For such correlations are normally expressed, in English at least, in temporal language such as

"Thunder always follows lightning." And while correlations involving objects and their properties are not usually expressed this way, they might be. So, for instance, one might say "A man is always an animal," meaning simply that all men are animals. If the same holds for Greek, then what Aristotle intends when he says that necessary truths are ἀεί is that they are strictly universal.

15. It seems that Aristotle's inclusion of this sort of example in *Posterior Analytics* 2.11 (where his general aim is to show how explanations involving all three of the *Physics'* four "causes" that are present in the *Analytics* can be cast into the form of demonstrative syllogisms) leads him for the first time to think of his highly related concepts of cause and explanation primarily in terms of *causal* (in the modern sense) relations between events, instead of logical relations between terms. This in turn leads him in *Posterior Analytics* 2.11 to begin asking "Humean" questions about the temporal relations between causes and their effects.

16. On this peculiar expression, which is evidently a counterpart to the expression the what-is-it in the *Posterior Analytics,* see Kosman (forthcoming).

17. I believe the same point would be expressed in the language of *Posterior Analytics* 1.4 by saying that grammatical capacity belongs to man not only κατὰ παντός, but also ἧ αὐτό (on which see chapter 3 above). This point is contested by Code (1986).

18. Perhaps these are connected through the concept of rationality.

19. Aristotle actually lists and discusses three types of propria besides the per se variety at *Topics* 128b15ff. These he describes as "temporary" (ποτέ), "relative" (πρὸς ἕτερον), and "permanent" (ἀεί). The special characteristics that distinguish these three types have no relevance to the present discussion, and will be ignored here.

20. This passage is discussed at length in chapter 1 above.

21. See also *De Anima* 1.1, 402a8–23.

22. Lennox (1987) does an excellent job of distinguishing this lateral form of demonstration (which he labels "A-explanations") from the two vertical types set out above (which Lennox does not distinguish from each other, but refers to indifferently as "B-explanations"). However, I believe he misinterprets Aristotle's arguments in *Posterior Analytics* 1.24, that demonstrations that are "universal" (τῆς καθόλου) are "better" (βελτίων; 85a15), or "more compelling" (κυριωτέρα; 86a23), than those that are "particular" (τῆς μέρος), to imply some preference on Aristotle's part for A-explanations over B-explanations. In fact, the main point of this chapter is really no more than an echo of *Posterior Analytics* 1.4 and 5: proving that a given attribute (in Aristotle's example *having angles equal to two right angles*) belongs to a certain kind (*isosceles triangle*), when the attribute in question also belongs necessarily to a wider kind (in this case, *triangle*), is epistemologically inferior to (and indeed depends upon) a "universal" proof that the attribute belongs to the whole of that wider kind. This, I take it, is just a restatement of the requirement of *Posterior Analytics* 1.4 that a complete demonstration must rest exclusively on premises that are extensionally immediate (or ἧ αὐτό, as

that expression was explained in chapter 3 above). This does not affect what I see as Lennox's correct and very important insight that Aristotle's later biological works (most especially, the *Historia Animalium*) display a pronounced preference for lateral explanations involving coextensive properties and codifferentiae.

23. Mure (1928).

24. This model is applied to Aristotle's *Physics* in chapter 1 of Waterlow (1982).

25. This assumption is entailed by a principle adhered to in the *Organon* (e.g., at *Topics* 1.15.107b19–26), but perhaps dropped in the biological works, that differentiating characteristics can apply only homonymously (usually analogously) across natural kinds.

26. If this is substantially correct, there remains the question of why Aristotle himself does not draw this connection explicitly, and why for that matter he does virtually nothing to indicate he is even aware that the two types of statements are superficially unlike one another. This I believe is just one of many symptoms of the fact that the theory of demonstration as a whole is intended to apply equally well both to natural sciences like biology and exact sciences like geometry (where by "equally" I mean that Aristotle is not willing to treat one of these types as paradigmatically demonstrative, and the other as a degenerate type). For ἐπὶ τὸ πολύ truths, while quite frequent in natural sciences, have no place at all in mathematics, whereas Aristotle's usual examples indicate that predications of per se propria are closely associated in his mind with mathematical proofs. Hence, I suggest that because his general policy is to stress the similarities between the two kinds of science (if, indeed, he even recognizes them as two distinct kinds in any important sense) and to underplay their differences, he is reluctant to attach much importance to what he regards as a superficial difference between the two sorts of predication.

27. As was argued in chapter 2, these must be genuine *predications*, i.e., referential universals, and not just Platonistic meaning assumptions.

CHAPTER 7: DEMONSTRATION AND NEGATION

1. By "negative predications," I am referring here and below to sentences stating that their subjects do not have the properties denoted by their respective predicates. That is, they are to be understood as involving the "internal" negation of a predicate, or perhaps of the copula. No contentions in this paper would be affected materially by making a finer distinction, clearly recognized by Aristotle in *De Interpretatione* 10 and *Prior Analytics* 1.46, between negating a predicate and negating the attachment of a predicate to a subject. Both of these are to be contrasted sharply with *denials,* or what have sometimes been called "sentence negations," which involve the "external" negation of some affirmative sentence (or proposition).

2. I thank James Lennox for this example.

3. Plato's views about this problem and his ways of dealing with it in the *Sophist* are discussed in some detail in Ferejohn (1989).

4. Moravcsik (1962 and 1973) tries to resist understanding Plato's objections to such divisions as having any essential connection with the use of negative concepts or expressions, insisting instead that the distinction relied upon in these passages is simply that between natural and artificial delineations. This view, which is compelled by Moravcsik's wider interpretation of the *Sophist,* is undermined by his own admission (1962, 72) that the most natural interpretation of *Statesman* 262D–E is the one he rejects.

5. Alexander, *in Metaphysica* 81, 3–4. Though Aristotle's worries about the meaning of negative predicates arise during a critical discussion of the Platonic Ideas, one may assume they apply *mutatis mutandis* to his own theory of predication on which *Aristotelian* universals are taken as the denotations of general terms.

6. There is some evidence to suggest that this view is shared by Alexander: "For 'not-man' is true of the horse and the dog, and of everything else besides the man, both existent and non-existent (ὄντων τε καὶ μὴ ὄντων). For it applies to both wood and stone, *to both centaur and chimera,* to what is utterly insubstantial, *to what nowise nohow is* (τοῦ μηδαμῇ μηδαμῶς ὄντος)" (*In Metaphysica* 80.17ff. alt.).

7. The absolute extreme of this sort of case is one where the background field is taken as all subjects of discourse, including nonexistents; cf. *De Interpretatione* 2, and *Peri Ideon* 80.17ff.

8. Lee (1972) incorrectly assumes that all varieties of meaning deficiency are "infectious" in the sense that any such defect of a part of a compound expression will necessarily be visited upon the whole. Hence: "each determinate Part of Otherness is opposed to some determinate Form and . . . its determinacy really *is* that of the Form to which it is directed . . ." (284–85, note 25, emphasis in original). In fact, given a constant background set, the determinacy of a negative term is *inversely* related to that of its affirmative component. I believe this confusion is ultimately rooted in Lee's overplaying of the knowledge analogy at 257C–D to the extent that he has Plato holding that each part of difference derives not just its determinate nature (and consequently its nameworthiness) but also *its very existence* from its correlated Form together with the Form of Difference (much as one might hold that arithmetic owes its existence to the faculty of knowledge and the field of numbers). This leads Lee to construe the *not-beautiful* as a sort of second-order intension which is somehow constructed out of, or as Lee puts it, "constituted by," the interweaving of Beauty and Difference (286). To the contrary, I maintain that the *not-beautiful* is simply the class of independently existing Forms that share the distinction of being different from and opposed to Beauty. If asked whether this interpretation of Plato is intensional or extensional, I would reply that the question is misdirected. It is most certainly not intensional in the sense employed by Lee (293); it insists that every term (positive or negative) signifies some Form or class of Forms and not some mysterious "specific negative intension" (293). Yet my interpretation is intensional insofar as Forms themselves are

classified as intensional entities, and insofar as it recognizes that Plato would never endorse a nominalistic analysis of "Socrates is not beautiful," on which the sentence merely places Socrates outside the class of beautiful things.

9. *De Interpretatione* 2.16a30–33, and 3.16b12–16. Compare also *De Interpretatione* 10, 12, and 14, passim, with *Prior Analytics* 1.46, passim.

10. The specific condition for termhood mentioned at *De Interpretatione* 2.16a28–30 is that an expression must "become a [genuine] symbol" (γένηται σύμβολον), that is, something more than the "inarticulate noises" (ἀγράμματοι ψόφοι) of beasts (a29), and this seems quite clearly to be a condition on meaningfulness. Consequently, it is a reasonable inference that Aristotle's grounds for disqualifying indefinite expressions as nouns and verbs in the strict sense is that they do not fully satisfy this condition, and we may speculate that he sees this shortcoming as due to their semantic fragmentation.

11. For Aristotle's advice on how this defect may be avoided, see his discussion in *Prior Analytics* 1.27 and *Posterior Analytics* 2.13 on the selection of *immediate* demonstrative premises.

12. See chapter 7, note 1 above.

13. In the face of the apparent conflict between these remarks and those from *De Interpretatione* and *Prior Analytics* considered earlier, I believe that the best course is to interpret Aristotle's attitude toward negative predicates as one of deep and persistent ambivalence. To be sure, he never makes any hard and fast distinction between formal and semantic considerations, but there is nonetheless a point to seeing the passages in question as dividing roughly along those lines. Since he recognizes that there are some perfectly unproblematic (because adequately restricted) occurrences of negative predicates, he is not ready to banish them altogether from his theory of predication. Accordingly, they are permitted in contexts (such as most of *De Interpretatione* and the *Prior Analytics*) where his aim is merely to set out the *formal conditions* on predication or logical inference. On the other hand, the issue of semantic fragmentation (and how to avoid it) naturally comes to the surface in passages (such as *Posterior Analytics* 78b25–30) dealing with such topics as meaning and explanation, where it is therefore evident that Aristotle is considering various of these forms under interpretation. (For instance, in the example given at 78b25–30, the form Camestres is considered under the interpretation, A=animal, B=breather, C=wall.) Thus, to record an Aristotelian distinction for which the author himself has no set terminology, we might say that he regards the use of negative predicates as permissible from a purely syntactical point of view but as in need of special semantical treatment to preserve significance.

14. The one exception Aristotle makes to this is the case of a subaltern science, where the premises used in a demonstration in one science are proved in some superordinate science, such as when arithmetical results are used in harmonics (76a10–11), or geometrical results are used in optics (78b35–39). On this relation of subordination among sciences, see Ferejohn (1980).

15. Incidentally, it is quite possible that Aristotle has parallel reasons for pro-

hibiting applications of so-called nonlogical axioms across different genera, even though these principles do not generally involve negative predication. For example, his insistence that the principle "Equals taken from equals yield equals," can only be used in restricted demonstrative contexts (e.g., as pertaining to equal numbers, or to lines of equal length) can be seen to reflect a concern that, if the term *equal* were taken to denote anything whatever in the category of Quantity, it would be too wide to possess a determinate meaning.

Bibliography

Ackrill, J. L., trans. 1963. Aristotle's *Categories and On Interpretation* (translation and notes). Oxford.

Barnes, J. 1969. "Aristotle's Theory of Demonstration." *Phronesis* 14: 123–52. Reprinted in *Articles on Aristotle*, vol. 1, *Science*. Edited by J. Barnes, M. Schofield, and R. Sorabji. London, 1975.

———. 1981. "Proof and the Syllogism" in *Aristotle on Science: The Posterior Analytics. Proceedings of the Eighth Symposium Aristotelicum*. Edited by E. Berti. Padua and New York.

Barnes, J., trans. 1975. *Aristotle's Posterior Analytics* (translation and notes). Oxford.

Bonitz, H. 1870. *Index Aristotelicus*. Berlin.

Burnyeat, M. 1970. "The Material and Sources of Plato's Dream." *Phronesis* 15: 101–22.

———. 1981. "Aristotle on Understanding Knowledge." In *Aristotle on Science: The Posterior Analytics. Proceedings of the Eighth Symposium Aristotelicum*. Edited by E. Berti. Padua and New York.

Cherniss, H. 1944. *Aristotle's Criticism of Plato and the Academy*. Baltimore.

Code, A. 1986. "Aristotle's Treatment of a Basic Logical Principle 1." *Canadian Journal of Philosophy* 16(3).

Cohen, S. M. 1971. "Socrates on the Definition of Piety: *Euthyphro* 10A–11B." *Journal of the History of Philosophy* 9: 1–13. Reprinted in *Socrates: Critical Essays*. Edited by G. Vlastos. Garden City, 1971, 158–76.

Dancy, R. 1975. "On Some of Aristotle's First Thoughts About Substance." *Philosophical Review* 84: 338–73.

Ferejohn, M. 1976. "Essentialism in Aristotle's Organon." Ph.D. dissertation, University of California, Irvine.

———. 1980. "Aristotle on Focal Meaning and the Unity of Science." *Phronesis* 25: 117–28.

———. 1981. "Aristotle on Necessary Truth and Logical Priority." *American Philosophical Quarterly* 18: 285–94.

——— 1982. "Definition and the Two Stages of Aristotelian Demonstration." *Review of Metaphysics* 36: 375–95.

———. 1984. "Socratic Virtue as the Parts of Itself." *Philosophy and Phenomenological Research* 44: 377–88.

———. 1989. "Plato and Aristotle on Negative Predication and Semantic Fragmentation." *Archiv fur Geschichte der Philosophie* 40.

———. Unpublished. "Aristotle on Snubness and the Definition of Composites."

Fine, G. 1979. "Knowledge and *Logos* in the *Theaetetus*." *Philosophical Review* 88: 367–97.

Frede, M. 1978. "Individuen bei Aristoteles." *Antike and Abendland*. Reprinted in *Essays in Ancient Philosophy*, Minneapolis, 1987.

Furth, M. 1988. *Substance, Form, and Psyche: An Aristotelean Metaphysics*. Cambridge.

Geach, P. T. 1962. *Reference and Generality: An Examination of Some Medieval and Modern Theories*. Ithaca.

Grene, M. 1963. *A Portrait of Aristotle*. Chicago.

Hintikka, J. 1957. "Necessity, Universality, and Time in Aristotle." *Ajatus* 20: 65–90.

———. 1972. "On the Ingredients of an Aristotelian Science." *Nous* 6(1): 55–69.

———. 1973. *Time and Necessity: Studies in Aristotle's Theory of Modality*. Oxford.

Irwin, T. 1988. *Aristotle's First Principles*. Oxford.

Jacobs, W. "Aristotle on Nonreferring Subjects." *Phronesis* 24: 282–300.

Kahn, C. 1973. "On the Theory of the Verb, 'To Be.'" In *Logic and Ontology*. Edited by M. Munitz.

———. 1981. "The Role of *Nous* in the Cognition of First Principles in *Posterior Analytics* II 19." In *Aristotle on Science: The Posterior Analytics. Proceedings of the Eighth Symposium Aristotelicum*. Edited by E. Berti. Padua and New York.

Kneale, W. 1936. "Is Existence a Predicate?" *Proceedings of the Aristotelian Society 1936*. Reprinted in *Readings in Philosophical Analysis*. Edited by H. Feigl and W. Sellars. New York, 1949.

Kosman, L. A. 1973. "Understanding, Explanation, and Insight in Aristotle's *Posterior Analytics*." In *Exegesis and Argument: Studies in Greek Philosophy Presented to Gregory Vlastos. Phronesis* suppl. vol. 1. Edited by E. Lee, A. Mourelatos, and A. Rorty.

———. Forthcoming. "Aristotle's Essences and Aristotelian Essentialism."

Kung, J. 1977. "Aristotle on Essence and Explanation." *Philosophical Studies* 31: 361–83.

Lear, J. 1980. *Aristotle's Logical Theory*. Cambridge.

Lee, E. N. 1972. "Plato on Not-Being in the *Sophist*." *Philosophical Review* 81: 267–304.

Lennox, J. 1987. "Divide and Explain: The *Posterior Analytics* in Practice." In *Philosophical Issues in Aristotle's Biology*. Edited by A. Gotthelf and J. Lennox.

Lesher, J. 1973. "The Meaning of *Nous* in the *Posterior Analytics*." *Phronesis* 18.

Lukasiewicz, J. 1957. *Aristotle's Syllogistic from the Standpoint of Modern Logic*. 2d edition. Oxford.

Mansion, S. 1976. *Le jugement d'Existence chez Aristote*. 2d edition. Louvain.

———. 1981. "La Signification de l'Universal d'apres An. Post. I 1." In *Aristotle on Science: The Posterior Analytics. Proceedings of the Eighth Symposium Aristotelicum*. Edited by E. Berti. Padua and New York.

Matthews, G. 1982. "Accidental Unities." In *Language and Logos*. Edited by M. Nussbaum and M. Schofield, Cambridge.

Mignucci, M. 1981. "Hos Epi To Polu et Necessaire dans la Conception Aristotelicienne de la Science." In *Aristotle on Science: The Posterior Analytics. Proceedings of the Eighth Symposium Aristotelicum*. Edited by E. Berti. Padua and New York.

Modrak, D. 1987. *Aristotle: The Power of Perception*. Chicago.

Moore, G. E. 1936. "Is Existence a Predicate?" *Proceedings of the Aristotelian Society 1936*. Reprinted in *Logic and Language*. 2d series. Edited by A. Flew. Oxford 1955.

Moravcsik, J. 1962. "Being and Meaning in the *Sophist*." *Acta Philosophica Fennica* 14: 23–78.

———. 1967. "Aristotle's Theory of Categories." In *Aristotle: Critical Essays*. Edited by J. Moravcsik. Garden City, 1967.

———. 1973. "The Anatomy of Plato's Divisions." In *Exegesis and Argument: Studies in Greek Philosophy Presented to Gregory Vlastos. Phronesis* suppl. vol. 1. Edited by E. Lee, A. Mourelatos, and A. Rorty.

Mure, G. R. G. 1928. Aristotle: *Posterior Analytics*. Oxford.

Nehamas, A. 1983. "*Episteme* and *Logos* in Plato's Later Thought." *Archiv fur Geschichte der Philosophie* 65: 11–36.

Owen, G. E. L. 1961. "*Tithenai Ta Phainomena*." In *Aristote et les Problemes de la Methode*. Edited by S. Mansion, Louvain. Reprinted in *Aristotle: Critical Essays*. Edited by J. Moravcsik. Garden City, 1967; and *Articles on Aristotle*, vol. 1, *Science*. Edited by J. Barnes, M. Schofield, and R. Sorabji. London, 1975.

———. 1965a. "Inherence." *Phronesis* 10: 97–105.

———. 1965b. "The Platonism of Aristotle." *Proceedings of the British Academy* 51: 125–50.

Patzig, G. 1969. *Aristotle's Theory of the Syllogism*. Dordrecht.

Quine, W. 1960. *Word and Object*. Cambridge, Mass.

Roberts, J. 1982. "Being, Not-Being, and Falsity in Plato's Sophist." Ph.D. dissertation, University of Pittsburgh.

Ross, W. D. 1949. *Aristotle's Prior and Posterior Analytics*. Oxford.

Russell, B. 1905. "On Denoting." *Mind* 14: 479–93.

Smith, R. 1982. "The Syllogism in *Posterior Analytics* I." *Archiv fur Geschichte der Philosophie* 64: 113–35.

――――. 1986. "Immediate Propositions and Aristotle's Proof Theory." *Ancient Philosophy* 6: 47–68.

Solmsen, F. 1929. *Die Entwicklung der Aristotelischen Logik und Rhetorik*. Berlin.

Sorabji, R. 1980. *Necessity, Cause, and Blame: Perspectives on Aristotle's Theory*. Ithaca.

Tredennick, H., trans. 1938. Aristotle's *Posterior Analytics*. Loeb Classical Library. Cambridge, Mass., and London.

Waterlow, S. 1982. *Nature Change and Agency in Aristotle's Physics*. Oxford.

White, N. 1972. "Origins of Aristotle's Essentialism." *Review of Metaphysics* 26: 57–85.

Index